Social Media and Civic Engagement

History, Theory, and Practice

Synthesis Lectures on Human-Centered Informatics

Editor

John M. Carroll, *Penn State University*

Human-Centered Informatics (HCI) is the intersection of the cultural, the social, the cognitive, and the aesthetic with computing and information technology. It encompasses a huge range of issues, theories, technologies, designs, tools, environments, and human experiences in knowledge work, recreation and leisure activity, teaching and learning, and the potpourri of everyday life. The series publishes state-of-the-art syntheses, case studies, and tutorials in key areas. It shares the focus of leading international conferences in HCI.

Social Media and Civic Engagement: History, Theory, and
Practice Scott P. Robertson

ISBN: 978-3-031-01095-8 Paperback
ISBN: 978-3-031-02223-4 PDF
ISBN: 978-3-031-00203-8 Hardcover
ISBN: 978-3-031-03351-3 ePub

DOI 10.1007/978-3-031-02223-4

A Publication in the Springer series
SYNTHESIS LECTURES ON HUMAN-CENTERED INFORMATICS, #40
Series Editors: John M. Carroll, Penn State University

Series ISSN: 1946-7680 Print   1946-7699 Electronic

Social Media and Civic Engagement

History, Theory, and Practice

Scott P. Robertson
University of Hawaii at Manoa

SYNTHESIS LECTURES ON HUMAN-CENTERED INFORMATICS #40

ABSTRACT

Social media platforms are the latest manifestation in a series of sociotechnical innovations designed to enhance civic engagement, political participation, and global activism. While many researchers started out as optimists about the promise of social media for broadening participation and enhancing civic engagement, recent events have tempered that optimism. As this book goes to press, Facebook is fighting a battle over the massive disclosure of user information during the 2016 U.S. presidential campaign, social analytics company Cambridge Analytica is being revealed as a major player in micro profiling voters in that same election, bots and fake news factories are undermining democratic discourse via social media worldwide, and the president of the United States is unnerving the world as a stream-of-consciousness Twitter user.

This book is a foundational review of current research on social media and civic engagement organized in terms of history, theory, practice, and challenges. History reviews how researchers and developers have continuously pushed the envelope to explore technology enhancements for political and social discourse. Theory reveals that the use of globally-networked social technologies touches many fields including political science, sociology, psychology, media studies, network science, and more. Practice is examined through studies of political engagement both in democratic situations and in confrontational situations. Challenges are identified in order to find ways forward.

For better or worse, social media for civic engagement has come of age. Citizens, politicians, and activists are utilizing social media in innovative ways, while bad actors are discovering possibilities for spreading dissent and undermining trust. We are at a sobering inflection point, and this book is your foundation for understanding how we got here and where we are going.

KEYWORDS

social media, civic engagement, social capital, digital cities, smart cities, urban informatics, digital activism, protest

Contents

Preface

At this moment, Facebook is fighting a battle over a massive disclosure of personal information about essentially all of its users during the 2016 U.S. presidential campaign; the social analytics company Cambridge Analytica is being revealed as a major player in microprofiling voters in that same election; the role of Russian bots and fake news factories in undermining democratic discourse in social media worldwide is being revealed; and the president of the U.S. is unnerving the world as a frequent stream-of-consciousness Twitter user. It is basically impossible to keep up with the rapid changes that the internet in general, and social media applications in particular, are bringing to the arenas of political discourse and civic engagement. Meanwhile, the Pew Internet and American Life Project generates a new report on social media use just about every week, and every HCI, CSCW, sociotechnical, and digital government conference brings on a slew of papers on exactly the topic of this book. This has made writing about social media and civic engagement a challenging task.

The first impression that many readers will probably have in browsing the contents is, "What about X?," where X is the latest thing that happened after mid-2018. Consequently, my strategy here is to bring together research to date on the internet, social media, and civic life that will be somewhat foundational to understanding this rapidly changing field. The book, therefore, concentrates heavily on both history and theory, in addition to practice. History because we got to where we are after many iterations of lively experimentation with community-oriented ICTs. In every technology cycle, researchers and developers pushed the envelope to see how technology could augment and enhance political and social discourse. It is enlightening to see what has endured, what has disappeared, and what has morphed. Theory because the use of globally networked social technologies for political discourse touches so many interesting, theory-rich fields: political science, sociology, psychology, media studies, network science, and more. No matter what happens in the realm of technology, theory will always apply in a novel way. So, it is important to understand how these theories apply in new sociotechnical contexts and, in turn, to see how theory is impacted by novel perspectives.

I have chosen to examine studies of engagement in two major categories: political engagement in democratic situations and political engagement in confrontational situations. Both are about changing the way things are, which is why we engage in political discourse in the first place. Social media has been up to the task of assisting with change in both cases, but in very different ways.

The book ends with challenges, which seem at times to overwhelm the opportunities. I began my research in this area a little over ten years ago, which just about tracks the lifespan of social media. Like many (not all), I started out as an optimist about the promise of social media for broadening participation and enhancing civic engagement. At this moment in time, however, it can seem more like a nightmare, as bad actors discover the possibilities of social platforms and related technologies. In fact, I think we are at a sobering inflection point, probably the same one that is encountered by all technology optimists as their favorite tools enter the larger sphere of public use. For better or worse, social media for civic engagement has "come of age."

This book will hopefully serve as a guidepost for going forward by showing where we have been, describing how we got here, and highlighting what is important in this vital area of research and practice.

Acknowledgments

This project could not have been completed without the endless patience, support, and inspiration provided by my wife, Mara Miller. She endured and successfully countered more bouts of "I can't do this" than should be expected of anyone. I am also eternally grateful to Jack Carroll, who has been my mentor and champion throughout my career.

CHAPTER 1

Introduction

1.1 TECHNOLOGY AND THE PUBLIC SPHERE

Historically, towns, villages, and cities had an area in which people gathered for common purpose—for example, to obtain food in the marketplace or gather water at the well. When people get together they like to talk politics, broadly defined, and in such public spaces, the state of political affairs and the foibles of the state's rulers have certainly always been discussed along with other shared concerns such as the weather and the latest gossip. Since the advent of democratic government, and especially as its inclusiveness has broadened, citizens have used public spaces to deliberate and make decisions about how their government, both local and national, works.

Most modern urban environments no longer have a central well or its physical equivalent. Many previously public activities have moved into the private domain. Supermarkets are not marketplaces, but rather commercial ventures designed to encourage shopping and discourage interaction. In many places, especially in the age of perceived global terrorism, modern public spaces such as transportation hubs and parks have restrictions on congregation and discourse among strangers. But in contemporary society a new kind of public space has emerged. Networked computing environments, ubiquitous mobile platforms, convergent media, and social software have combined to enable digital civic engagement and perhaps create new forms of civic participation.

While a small group may come to consensus through discussion amongst themselves, a larger group, and most certainly groups at the size of towns and nations, must develop organizational structures through which the expressions of individuals may flow to decision makers who are, in turn, empowered to make decisions, take actions, and enforce policies and practices. Thus, representative government and deliberative politics depend on the ability of individuals to express themselves using both information transfer and *communication* techniques that span distances and also more intimate *spaces* of some kind or another to allow for immediate deliberation and discourse.

Systems of messengers such as the ancient Greeks and the League of the Iroquois, and later the postal system riders of colonial America, allowed for the practice of collective decision making and governance at a distance. Such systems must support, on the one hand, delivery of information about the desires of individuals (collected in various ways) to a centralized location where they can be collected and considered by empowered representatives, and, on the other hand, delivery of the decisions of the representatives back to the people for action. Depending on the physical distribution of the polity, such communications were conducted on a time scale of weeks and months. But, in the contemporary period, communication technology has changed these processes considerably. The advent of the telegraph and telephone reduced the time scale for information transfer to mere seconds. The advent of social media has now reduced the time scale for transfer of information among members of a community, and between municipal or government representatives and their polities, to instantaneous.

In the West, with the advent of a proto-democratic tradition in ancient Greece came an official *space* for political discourse: the Agora. In the agoras of Greek city-states, citizens—a class largely limited to male land owners—gathered to hear proclamations, witness trials, hear philosophical lectures, and debate and vote on political and civic issues. Over time, as the concept of citizen has expanded, so too has the breadth of spaces dedicated to critical civic and political discourse.

Political theory has recently taken what Dryzek (2000) refers to as a deliberative turn, which refers to an emphasis on communication about political and civic matters, hence placing politics and engagement into a sphere of social activities. Effective political and civic deliberation is contingent upon the ability of the discourse to prompt reflection and ultimately result in a collective outcome. In fact, Dryzek felt even at the end of the millennium that the state of affairs was better described in terms of what he called *discursive democracy* (Dryzek, 1990), where discussion of many types—including not only rational and/or persuasive argument, but also sarcasm, humor, gossip, storytelling, appeal to emotion, and more—leads to reflection and in which individual states have less and less control over a discourse that is increasingly international. Introduce social media, a sociotechnical grab bag of every sort of rhetorical and discursive communication available, into this frame at the beginning of the new millenium, and social media's central role in reshaping civic and political life becomes obvious.

Jürgen Habermas (1989) famously traced the evolution of what he called the "public sphere" (discussed at length in Chapter 3) through 19th- and early 20th-century Europe as it expanded into a more bourgeois society of merchants and other middle-class citizens. He proposed that these citizens increasingly engaged in "rational-critical debate" in the cafes and salons that emerged, at least in part, for this purpose. In the age of the internet, many sociotechnical and political theorists have moved quickly to discuss the implications of a digitally mediated *public sphere* (Benkler, 2006; Boeder, 2005; Castells, 2009; Dahlberg, 2001; Dahlgren, 2005, 2009, 2016; Papacharissi, 2002, 2009, 2010; Poor, 2005), and this discussion evolves with the speed of digital innovation and contemporary cultural liquidity.

Today, although shaky at times, most democratic polities embrace at least the concept of participation of all classes. The advent of mass media in the 20th century has allowed for information to flow easily to such a wide swath of the public who might not otherwise find themselves in common spaces in which to engage in discourse. Many public and civic spaces in the current period, then, have become "de-physicalized." One of the many virtual spaces we inhabit includes space for public discourse, and the nature and use of such space is an ongoing topic of interest to scholars in communication, information science, political science, and other fields.

The appearance of social media and widespread social-media enhancements to a plethora of internet environments at the start of the 21st century has added a new twist to the contemporary understanding of civic participation. The advent of these tools, which are radically non-authoritarian when compared, for example, to television, have raised the question of whether a new era of civic engagement is underway. Papacharissi (2010) suggests that citizens today encounter civic society as a hybrid environment of overlapping private and public spheres and that citizenship itself is experienced in a highly fluid manner.

Technology utopians view the appearance of networked information sharing environments as an unrivaled democratizing force (Benkler, 2006; Nisbet, Stoycheff and Pearce, 2012; Rheingold, 2000; Stoycheff and Nisbet, 2014; Valenzuela, Park, and Key, 2009), which can both enhance the effectiveness of already engaged citizens (Bimber, 1999; DiMaggio et al, 2004; Krueger, 2002; Norris, 2000, 2001; Polat, 2005; Weber, Loumakis, and Bergman, 2003) and bring new citizens into the fold (Delli Carpini, 2000; Krueger, 2002; Ward, Gibson, and Lusoli, 2003; Weber, Loumakis, and Bergman, 2003). On the other hand, technology pessimists find that issues like inequitable access, surveillance, the viral spread of rumors and fake news, and the echo chamber of selected friends and hyper-targeted media preempt the usefulness of digital networks for democratic discourse (Gerhards and Schäfer, 2010; Kaufhold, Valenzuela and De Zúñiga, 2010; Putnam, 1995, 2000; Stroud, 2008; Sunstein, 2007). Of course, the truth is much more nuanced and complicated, requiring consideration of what kinds of people are using which platforms in which contexts for what purposes (Boullianne, 2009). In this book, we will examine the use of recently emerging social information and computing technologies as they have been appropriated for use in civic, political, and other contexts of public participation.

Voida et al. (2014) find that literature on e-government systems tends to be grouped into three values themes. First is the value of *access*, or the ability of citizens to acquire information and have influence on their governments. The second is *efficiency*, a value that stresses cost-cutting and tame-saving features of digital services. Finally, the value of education stresses how e-government systems can increase awareness and understanding of civic and governmental processes, hence making citizens more informed, reflective, and empowering them to be more active in their civic contexts.

1.2   CIVIC ENGAGEMENT

It makes sense to begin by asking what we mean by the term *civic engagement*. There have been many takes on defining what civic engagement means, but an overview of several reveals that there are commonalities.

The Center for Information on Civic Learning and Engagement (CIRCLE), which studies youth engagement, divides civic engagement into three categories (Keeter et al., 2002):

- Civic activities

- Electoral activities

- Political voice

Civic activities include volunteering for non-electoral organizations, membership in groups or associations, participation in fundraising for causes, and community problem solving. *Electoral activities* include voting on a regular basis; persuading others; displaying buttons, signs, or stickers; making campaign contributions; and volunteering in political campaigns or for political organizations. *Political voice* involves contacting officials or media, protesting, petitioning, canvassing, and engaging in political actions such as boycotts.

Korn and Voida (2015) distinguish between two major forms of civic engagement as viewed through the lens of human-computer interaction. In the first, designers and researchers work within mainstream political contexts, for example to create e-government services, to make voting more straightforward and accessible, to seek input from citizens on government actions, and to enable and foster debate and deliberation. In the second, designers and researchers work outside of mainstream political channels, for example to support the work of activists, non-governmental organizations, protesters, and others in non-official capacities.

Another approach to understanding civic engagement is to focus on processes involved in various stages of action and on the contexts that enable and influence the effectiveness of these processes. For example, Gordon, Baldwin-Philippi, and Balestra (2013) delineate three major activities that constitute most forms of civic engagement:

- Acquiring and processing information

- Voicing and debating opinions and beliefs

- Taking action

They point out that, although taking action is often considered to be the most desirable form of civic engagement, acquiring information and debating issues are equally important and serve to inform action. This becomes critically important when we consider social media, especially as it has evolved from an information-sharing environment into a more active participation environment.

Along similar lines, Norris (2001) believes that civic engagement with regard to politics entails three important factors:

- Political knowledge

- Political trust

- Political participation

Political knowledge is what people learn about political issues, candidates, and affairs from consuming media and talking with others. *Political trust* is the sense of support for political institutions and political actors. *Political participation* involves the various ways that citizens take action to influence how government works or to impact the decision making of politicians. Norris calls out trust because it can be seen as having an impact on confidence in government systems and therefore it serves as a facilitator of participation. Researchers have extensively examined how the internet shapes all of these factors, perhaps leading to increased knowledge, increased trust, and greater participation (Kenski and Stroud, 2010).

Several researchers suggest that computer-mediated interactions have positive effects on community engagement and civic involvement (Donath and boyd, 2004; Hampton and Wellman, 2003; Kavanaugh et al., 2005; Resnick, 2001). For example, internet users are more likely than non-internet users to be involved in civic and political activities such as attending a political rally, trying to influence a vote, and actually voting or reporting intention to vote—and frequent Facebook users are even more highly engaged in these civic/political activities (Hampton et al., 2011; Raine and Smith, 2012). Facebook users maintain many types of relationships within the site and seem to gain and maintain social capital from its use (Ellison, Steinfield, and Lampe, 2007; Resnick, 2001; Wellman et al., 2001).

So, "civic engagement" can be construed as any activity performed by people that is relevant to their community, society, culture, nation, or to issues of global citizenship. This covers both active and passive forms of engagement, although these stances toward engagement can be hard to distinguish from each other. For example, an individual might read the posts of a politician and the comments of other citizens on a social media platform, but never post themselves. While this *lurking* behavior is often classified as passive, it does require that the individual find the material and make decisions about what to look at. Presumably, it is also performed for a purpose related to civic participation, such as learning about a candidate and understanding their positions or judging their popularity.

Perhaps we should view participation as varying on continua across at least two axes: intensity of discussion and intensity of action. Intensity of discussion refers to the content of what is posted on social media. Instead of a dichotomy of participation (posting something) versus non-participation (lurking), we may view participation intensity on an ordinal scale anchored on one end by lurking and on the other by continuous engagement with many others in prolonged discourse. With regard to action, a similar ordinal scale exists with people who take in information at one end and people who participate in real-world activity such as voting, petition signing, demonstrating, and participating in revolt on the other. Social media affords civic engagement by users in all parts of this intensity-action space.

1.3   SOCIAL MEDIA

In this book, we are concerned primarily with the impact of *social media* on civic engagement. Although bulletin boards and other community-oriented media have been around for a while, social media as we know it today began at the start of the 21st century. The earliest pure social networking sites—Friendster, LinkedIn, and MySpace—were launched in 2002–2003. The first YouTube video was uploaded in 2005. Twitter was started in 2006. Facebook opened to a non-restrictive membership also in 2006. Other rapidly growing social media platforms such as Reddit, Instagram, and Snapchat are even younger.

A definitional part of the concept of Web 2.0, social media includes computing platforms that allow users to interact with each other, to share and augment media content such as news articles, and to post, comment on, and respond to media of all kinds, including text, images, video, and music. A critical feature of social media is that it is a *prosumer* environment, involving all participants in both the production and consumption aspects of its use (Ritzer and Jurgenson, 2010). Thus, the content of social media is largely user-generated, although users now post journalistic media, news, and other professionally produced material as well, and social media platforms have evolved a much more seamless integration of these different types of materials. Similarly, while there are different platforms for different media types—Instagram for pictures and YouTube for videos, for example—social media sites are also now moving to integration of material across platforms and are also supporting multiple media types within their own environments. The typical newsfeed on Facebook, by far the most popular social media environment, will contain text posts from friends and friends-of-friends; pictures from friends and acquaintances; embedded videos from friends, organizations, and professional sources; embedded news and magazine stories from multiple sources; jokes and memes from friends and organizations; updates on travel; targeted advertising; links and reposts from microblogs like Twitter or image platforms like Instagram; and so on.

All of these features may be reacted to instantly with a range of emotional expressions and may be commented on in a threaded comment section with text or any other content of the types mentioned above. In other words, these environments have become complex, multifaceted, multimedia, multisource information firehoses that mix social, commercial, civic, and other matters mercilessly. They are accessible at any time through mobile devices and visited multiple times per day by literally billions of users.

Social media can be a stand-alone environment or platform in which users maintain a friend, acquaintance, and/or follower network, and typically intermingle content sharing and information dissemination activities in multiple spheres (e.g., entertainment, politics, news, etc.). Social media can also be an added feature to other application environments, for example as a commenting area on news stories or videos, or as a Twitter feed embedded in a web application. Seamless integration of social networking applications with content-supplying applications has been achieved by many popular platforms. Many traditional online media outlets provide liking and sharing buttons that instantly move content into a social media stream where it can be immediately viewed by friends and followers, embellished, and rebroadcast throughout the network. Most recently, traditional news outlets such as the *New York Times* have entered into deals to integrate their content directly into social media feeds without the need for sharing. This widespread integration of social media functions within other applications, in conjunction with the fact that many users maintain an open, background social media application while doing other things on the internet, makes it difficult to assess exactly when internet users are engaged in social media activity, or more accurately it makes it difficult to assess when they are *not* engaged in social media activity. In fact, it is probably best to assume that for many internet users social networking is a constant state, either potential or realized.

The Pew Research Center's Internet and American Life Project has been tracking multiple aspects of the use of social media since its inception. Sixty-five percent of American adults now use social networking sites (Perrin, 2015). The highest usage is by younger people in the age range of 18–29 (90%), although other age groups also report moderate to high usage (77% of 30–49 year olds, 51% of 50–64 year olds, 35% of people over 65 years of age), and of course the growth rate is dramatic. Women use social networking sites slightly more than men (women = 68%, men = 62%). More highly educated individuals with higher household incomes are greater users of social media, however no educational or income group falls under 50% usage of social networking platforms anymore. Greenwood, Perrin, and Duggan (2016) report extremely high use of multiple social media sites among online Americans, with Facebook leading the pack at a usage rate of 79% of all online Americans. Instagram, Pintrest, LinkedIn, and Twitter follow with usage rates of 32%, 31%, 29%, and 24% respectively. Three-quarters of Facebook users visit the site every day, and half of them visit it multiple times per day. More than half of social media users visit multiple sites.

The advent of social media was a game changer for community computing. Suddenly, community activities that designers had been trying to support in various civic computing environments were available for appropriation in a handful of popular social networking sites. Many community, civic, and even governmental interactive functions are now accomplished via integrated social media sites.

Social media platforms have been implicated in a variety of political movements such as the 2011 Occupy Wall Street movement in the U.S. (Caren and Gaby, 2011); the 2010–2012 Arab-Spring related uprisings throughout the Middle East including Tunisia (Kavanaugh et al., 2016; Wulf et al., 2013b), spreading to Egypt (Khamis and Vaughn, 2011; Lim, 2012; Tufeckci and Wilson, 2012) and Turkey (Dincelli, Hong, and DePaula, 2016); Karkın et al., 2015; Varol et al., 2014), and elsewhere (Howard and Hussain, 2011); occupied West Bank villages (Wulf et al., 2013a); and other significant populist movements globally (Shirky, 2011). They have played increasingly important roles in elections in mature democracies (Vitak et al., 2011), and are playing significant roles in connecting citizens to each other and to their governments in many emerging democracies

(Morozov, 2009). Social media is used increasingly as an important part of digital government initiatives throughout the world. Barak Obama established the @POTUS Twitter tag in early 2015 and became the first sitting American president to join the Facebook social network later that same year. Manipulation of social media to influence elections is one of the biggest stories of the 2016 U.S. presidential election, and as of this writing (2018), a newly elected president Donald Trump is blazing a trail as an everyday user of the Twitter microblogging site (@realDonaldTrump) to express thoughts, emotions, and reactions that seem spontaneous and un-vetted.

In addition to direct use for the activities of civic engagement, social media now plays an important role in news dissemination, and hence in information gathering relevant to political action and political opinion. Sixty-two percent of American adults get news from social media sources (Gottfried and Shearer, 2016). Again, the role of news varies considerably depending on the social media site in question. Reddit, Facebook, and Twitter provide the greatest opportunities for exposure to news and information within their platforms, with 70% of Reddit users, 66% of Facebook users, and 59% of Twitter users reporting that they get news from these respective platforms. Thirty-one percent of Tumblr users report getting news from that site. Other sites fall well under 25%. The dominance of Facebook as a social media platform, combined with its large role as a source of news, make it the primary social media source of news for American adults (Greenwood, Perrin, and Duggan, 2016). In earlier reports, a little more than one third (36%) of social networking site users say that these platforms are important for keeping up with political news in particular (Raine and Smith, 2012). Again, at the current time (2018), the organized creation and dissemination of "fake news" to influence political opinion is under increased scrutiny.

Research on the use of social media by citizens to interact with government has focused on three modes of information dissemination: one-way push, two-way pull, and networking (Meijer and Thaens, 2013; Mergel, 2013a). Despite the advent of social media, research to date has shown that government use of social media is largely one-way, with many local governments still using a "push" model in which information flows from the government to the citizen (Mergel, 2013b; Mossberger, Wu, and Crawford, 2013). DePaula and Dincelli (2016) characterized Facebook posts of municipal-level government agencies in the U.S. to be mainly push oriented (policy announcements and public service announcements), secondarily impression management oriented (marketing, political positioning, positive imagery and favorable publicity), in small amounts (<8%) networking oriented (calls for discussion, dialog, and volunteers), and in very small amounts (<3%) pull oriented (requests for feedback, fundraising).

1.4   ORGANIZATION

In Chapter 2, we trace some history of the use of information and computing systems (ICSs) in civic contexts. We divide this history into pre- and post-social periods since the emergence of social media can be seen as a revolutionary turn in the emergence and adoption of ICSs in civic and government contexts. In Chapter 3, we explore theories that arise in the literature frequently. Theories relevant to this book are highly interdisciplinary, coming from political science, sociology, network science, and informatics and information science. In Chapter 4, we take a tour of the many studies of social media and civic engagement, dividing them into engagements with the orderly democratic process and then engagements in situations of protest and resistance. In Chapter 5 we conclude by discussing challenges that have emerged.

CHAPTER 2

History

2.1 DIGITAL CITIES

We can ask to what degree digital cities and community networks are examples of civic engagement. While most have the goal of supporting community involvement, they all have something of a "Chamber of Commerce" quality to them in the sense that their primary goals are to connect businesses to citizens and to publicize and popularize the community to outsiders. The need for significant technical capital in terms of both money and infrastructure meant that large institutions such as telecoms, city governments, and universities needed to work together to make the digital cities a reality. These entities view the community and its needs differently than citizens might. In the next section, we explore the emergence of civic activities on platforms not designed specifically for this purpose and therefore without design constraints on activity.

Van Dijk (2012) identifies four distinct periods in the development of digital democracy: (1) *teledemocracy* in the 1980s as networked computing environments first appeared; (2) *virtual community* in the 1990s in which communities of interest and locality could interact and share (with an emphasis on replacing "lost community"); (3) *new democracy* at the turn of the century in which the global reach of the internet, the possibilities for mass participation became apparent; and (4) *Web 2.0* era as the dawn of social media and civic journalism made participatory environments prevalent. We focus in this book on the last era, however in this chapter we spend some time charting how we got here.

As soon as it became clear that information and computing systems would break out beyond large corporations and military and scientific applications, and that their uses were vastly broader than accounting, record keeping, and mathematical calculation, people began to imagine their use in civic and governmental realms. When document processing and hypertext emerged in the 1970s, an early dream was that public documents, which were printed at great cost and either mailed to citizens or kept in publicly accessible places such as post offices and libraries, could instead reside online. By the 1990s, community-level and city-level websites were appearing which informed citizens about and involved them in civic affairs. The so-called "digital cities" movement emerged at this time with many forward-thinking communities developing a cyber-presence for municipalities and their citizens. Often the metaphor was tied closely to real urban spaces, with a community being represented spatially, citizens having "home" pages, and navigation being accomplished by moving from place to place though the simulated environment.

The internet emerged from its development into broader common use in the 1980s, and almost immediately along with it came the dream that people could use it to form neighborhood, city, state, national, and transnational amalgams to pursue common ends. The phrase "digital city" was used to indicate the movement of city-level and community-level activities of civic life into the digital domain.

Van den Besselaar and Beckers (2005) trace the origin of the term "digital city" to the founding in 1993 of *De Digitale Stad* (DDS) in Amsterdam, widely considered to be the first attempt at creating a connected urban network with civic goals beyond simply experimenting with emerging technologies. DDS arose in an environment that had already appropriated the new technology of cable television for community access purposes. An amalgam of hackers and community activists embarked on the DDS project with the goal of offering universal internet access and developing applications that citizens could use to accomplish civic ends. According to van den Besselaar and Beckers (2005):

> *"The organizers wanted to introduce the Internet and its possibilities to a wider population by providing free access to the Internet, creating an electronic public domain for social and political debate and enabling free expression and social experimentation in cyberspace"* (p. 68).

One of the first accomplishments of DDS was to link politicians with citizens and to set up political discussion forums to support elections taking place in 1994. As far as I know, this is the first use of a digital network environment to support an election. Although it grew quickly at first, DDS had a difficult time transitioning through various phases of technological change, particularly the introduction of the World Wide Web, and the ultimate commercialization of the internet. The rise of commercial providers of competing services such as email and search tools eroded the large user base who focused primarily on these particular services.

A significant feature of DDS was its use of an urban metaphor to organize its services and features. DDS contained a "library," "post office," "city hall," "arts and culture center," "election center," special interest "cafes," and other virtual places. This metaphor was maintained when DDS switched from a text-based interface to a graphical interface, and the latter allowed designers to present the "digital city" spatially as a city map and to support "strolling" as a navigational metaphor. Users were encouraged to have a "house" in a virtual neighborhood, which was an early version of representing the self in cyberspace. While this drew considerable attention from researchers as an innovative and interesting experiment in virtual public space, it may have proved limiting both technically (there were limits on the number of houses and sizes of neighborhoods, for example) and in terms of the constraints of the metaphor with regard to imaginative new applications. An attempt to deploy a 3D interface to DDS and integrate it with live television was probably ahead of its time in the 1990s and resulted in a reduction in users who had the bandwidth and computing power to use DDS. By 2001, DDS had disappeared (see Van den Besselaar and Beckers, 2005 for an extensive history).

Several community network efforts with similarities to DDS appeared around the U.S. at about the same time (Schuler, 1994). Examples include Big Sky Telegraph, Berkeley Community Memory (Farrington and Pine, 1996), Santa Monica Public Electronic Network (Rogers, Collins-Jarvis, and Schmitz, 1994), Seattle Community Network (SCN), and Blacksburg Electronic Village (BEV). According to Yasuoka, Ishida, and Aurigig (2010), the earliest digital city was the Cleveland Free-Net, founded in 1986 as a research project within Case Western Reserve University.

The Cleveland Free-Net (CFN) was a local network initially not connected to the then-nascent internet. It provided email and online bulletin board services to its users, who numbered almost 160,000 by the time of its discontinuation in 1995. The evolution of the CFN was largely an experiment in technical capability, however it was also an early example of an information network in which the users played a significant role in producing its content. The founder of CFN, who also envisioned a "National Public Telecomputing Network" (NPTN) in advance of the fully realized internet, described several requirements for public networks (Schuler, 1994). They should be:

- community-based, such that everyone has a stake in the content;

- reciprocal, where users are both information consumers and producers;

- contribution-based, in which the content of forums is generated by users;

- unrestricted, allowing anyone to contribute anything (with limitations on harassing, criminal, or libelous content);

- accessible and inexpensive, to maximize equitable use; and

- modifiable, whereby the system and services themselves can be changed in a participatory manner by users.

As we will see, these requirements for community networks have interesting resonance with the requirements that political theorists place on open deliberative spaces. The founders of CFN encouraged developers of other "Free Nets" to measure desirable outcomes such as increased community cohesion; better-informed citizens; greater use of educational and training resources over the lifespan; and an "inclusive, ethical, and enlightened democracy."

The SCN is notable because, like DDS, many local activist groups were involved in its funding. Initially, an environmental group called Sustainable Seattle established a home page on the site, followed closely by a homeless women's network called the Homeless Network, and a feminist organization called BaseCamp Seattle. BaseCamp Seattle held early meetings combining technology education and awareness with political workshops (Silver, 2004). Growth of SCN was fast for the time, starting with 700 users in 1994 and growing to 13,000 in 1997 (Schuler, 1996).

The Blacksburg Electronic Village (BEV), launched in 1993, stands in stark contrast to many of the "free net" projects because of the extensive attention paid to it by behavioral and social scientists (Carroll, 2005). Like CFN, BEV was also a collaboration between a university, Virginia Polytechnic Institute and State University (Virginia Tech), and its surrounding community. The promise of BEV, and community networks in general, is reflected in this quote from an early research project:

> *"[C]ommunity networks are a potentially radical medium within which to manage community history: they augment the real, physical communities in which we live our fragmented lives by supporting distributed, asynchronous, personal interactions: we can get to the campfire or General Store anytime and anywhere"* (Carroll et al., 1995, p. 6).

Surveys taken during the early days of BEV showed that people's primary interests in the network were "learning and teaching, civic interests, social relations, support for work or business, consumer information, entertainment, and medical services" (Carroll and Rosson, 1996). When it was founded, BEV maintained a discussion forum for policies related to use of the network, however this forum quickly became a hub for discussion of civic issues such as downtown parking policies and for community issues such as restaurant reviews and birth announcements (Carroll and Rosson, 1996).

BEV initially had two primary goals, to connect citizens with government electronically and to help businesses create and utilize a digital presence (Carroll, 2005). The goal of connecting citizens with each other was not prominent at the outset, but as various local organizations began to develop presences on BEV, many community-building activities began to evolve. Carroll (2005) describes how senior groups, churches, and other organizations successfully occupied BEV and created social communities that might otherwise have not formed.

Early on BEV became a participatory project in which members built their own content. Eventually, as other user-driven content sites became prominent, BEV evolved into an organizational portal. Still, this DIY feature is often referenced as a reason for the long-term success of BEV (Carroll, 2005; Carroll and Rosson, 1996).

BEV successfully navigated the transition from a text-based network to a predominantly graphical network on the World Wide Web. While BEV itself never utilized a strict place-based metaphor such as DDS, a companion project called MOOsburg did graft a geographical coordinate system with landmarks and community meeting tools to the BEV infrastructure (Carroll et al., 2001), but this effort remained largely outside of the mainstream use of BEV.

BEV remained in service until 2015. Its take-down notice recognizes the fate of many early "digital city" and community network services, that commercial providers ultimately won the day:

"This transition recognizes the success of BEV in that many of the services that it has provided in a speculative, experimental context are now widely available from a variety of providers" (from the BEV Transition Announcement, http://www.bev.net/transition-announcement).

While early digital cities often made attempts to render their interfaces graphically, none went quite as far in this direction as Helsinki, Finland (Linturi, Koivunen, and Sulkanen, 1999) and Kyoto, Japan (Ishida and Isbister, 2000; Ishida, 2002). In these cases, attempts were made to create a digital urban experience using a virtual city environment in which government services, shopping opportunities, and interaction were enabled via avatars. Digital City Kyoto originated from NTT and Kyoto University in 1998. The concept was to create a virtual space that was isomorphic to the real city. The researchers imagined a three-layer architecture consisting of an information layer, interface layer, and interaction layer. In anticipation of the smart city concept, Digital City Kyoto was envisioned to have sensors and monitors on physical objects that would aggregate data and represent it in a visualization of real urban space. This information layer relied heavily on GIS data and address information to situate the user in a realistic visual depiction of the city. The interface layer generated 2D and 3D representations of space using real images. Finally, the interaction layer was intended to employ chat software for interactions among people through their avatars and chatbots for directing tours and helping in wayfinding.

2.2 E-GOVERNMENT PORTALS

In parallel with the digital cities movement, researchers and practitioners from the areas of political science and public policy have engaged in efforts to develop portals to local and national government services. Researchers began to explore the idea that governments and citizens could interact electronically almost at the birth of the internet (for example, see Braman, 1995; Stenberg, Ayres, and Kettinger, 1983). In general, their concerns were not with the formation of communities or necessarily citizen deliberation, but rather the opening of channels between government and citizens for information dissemination and transaction, productivity and cost impacts, the legal and bureaucratic issues involved in information sharing, matters of transparency and privacy, standards, relations among levels of government, intergovernmental (and even international) boundaries, and the lines between public and private interests in information management. Much of the literature on e-government was (and is) published in the information science literature and, more recently, government- and policy-related journals and conferences (Belanger and Carter, 2012). According to Grönlund and Horan (2005), the information systems field has dominated in conducting research and developing theory in the area of e-government systems (cf. Andersen and Henriksen, 2005; Grönlund, 2004).

Proponents of e-government systems argued from the beginning that they might bring fundamental changes to how government works. Fountain (2002) predicted that information technology in government would bring positive changes to social, economic, and political aspects of government. While adoption of new e-government systems has been consistent and widespread, positive impacts have been seen mostly in productivity and efficiency gains rather than in fundamental practices. In a significant overview of the adoption of information technologies in government, Kraemer and King (2006) concluded the following:

- "[T]echnology [is] useful in some cases of administrative reform, but only in cases where expectations for reform are already well-established. IT application does not cause reform."

- "IT application has brought relatively little change to organization structures, and seems to reinforce existing structures."

- "[T]he primary beneficiaries [of information technology] have been functions favored by the dominant political-administrative coalitions in public administrations, and not those of technical elites, middle managers, clerical staff, or ordinary citizens."

- "Government managers have a good sense of the potential uses of IT in their own interests, and in cases where their interests coincide with government interests, they push IT application aggressively."

In other words, the adoption of information technologies has been largely non-transformational.

Analysis and benchmarking of government portals (Rorissa, Demissie, and Pardo, 2011) and websites often distinguish between several levels of service, roughly as follows.

- Information dissemination from government to citizens (G2C).

- Rudimentary two-way communication between government and citizens such as e-mail (G2C and C2G).

- Online transaction processing, e.g., licensing, permitting, payments. In later stages voting and rulemaking (participation in legislation).

- Citizen engagement in highly interactive and collaborative endeavors in support of civic, governmental, and political activities (C2C, sometimes referred to as "government 2.0").

- Collaborative, open government (includes leveraging of citizen-generated data and crowdsourcing of civic solutions both in collaboration with, and independent of, government).

Bimber (2000) argued at the beginning of the century for abandonment of ideas like "cyber-democracy" or "e-government," which imply that a new of civic participation is emerging from use of the internet and other information technologies:

> "*Analysis of civic engagement might well proceed, I believe, by modeling a civic landscape that is growing increasingly information rich and communication intensive, rather than one that is permeated by one technology or another. Technologies change and evolve over time, of course, but the trend toward lower and lower marginal costs of information and communication will likely continue for the foreseeable future. If information technology is a cause, its proximate effect is to create societies that are in many ways more information rich and communication intensive, societies where the marginal cost of information and communication is very low. The question, then, becomes one of understanding the ultimate effects that follow from those new informational circumstances*" (Bimber, 2000, p. 331).

Bimber argues that instead of considering the internet to be revolutionary, we should consider it to be one in a long series of changes (albeit, a dramatic change) in the history of information management (Castells, 1996), and that research should focus on how organizations and individuals adapt their practices accordingly. Bimber's argument is that we should view changes in civic engagement in the era of the internet as an evolutionary adaptation to dramatic shifts in the global information ecology.

A significant feature of the internet, according to Bimber (2000), is the reduction in "information cost," or the reduction in resources required to produce and disseminate information broadly and swiftly. He predicted many outcomes with regard to political and civic participation, including:

- greater fragmentation and pluralism in the structure of civic engagement as information efforts become more specialized and focused;

- replacing of large political organizations that persist through multiple events (e.g., political parties) with more flexible, special-issue, and temporary ad-hoc groups;

- a rise in smaller political parties and reduction in the power of big parties;

- more rapid cycling of the political agenda and acceleration of the pace of the public agenda;

- a "deinstitutionalization" of civic life;

- a multiplication in opportunities for learning about civic issues and becoming involved in activism;

- a potential for limiting perception of the common public good as aggregates of special interests gain more of the public attention and set more of the public agenda; and

- a potential trade-off between liberty and deliberation about the common good.

Several researchers, in studies of use of electronic portals like BEV, found that early adopters tended to be more civic minded than those who began using civic components of the internet later (Kohut, 1999; Patterson and Kavanaugh, 2001; Kavanaugh and Patterson, 2001). They argue that increases in civic engagement and community involvement that seem to be internet related are actually a phase of technology adoption rather than a true change in behavior.

2.3   OPEN GOVERNMENT

As early as the 1950s it was recognized that data collected by the government was useful when aggregated across silos and also that it should be available to citizens (Parks, 1957). Political turmoil in the 1970s concerning leaked government documents (the Pentagon Papers in particular) created a lively discussion about citizens' "right to know" about information that the government collected or created (Ivester, 1977), a controversy that finds new relevance in the era of Wikileaks. Jaeger, Bertot, and Shuler (2010) argue that access to and dissemination of government data are core founding principles in the U.S., and many European countries have similarly found the right of citizens to government data to be fundamental (Gomes and Soares, 2014). The open data movement has seen successes in many countries, including the establishment of data.gov and the associated Open Government Directive promulgated by the Obama administration in the U.S., and Open Data Strategy for Europe (European Commission, 2013), a United Nations Statement on Open Government Data for Citizen Engagement (United Nations, 2013), and many others (Gomes and Soares, 2014; Zuiderwijk and Janssen, 2014a).

The significance of the open data movement for changing the relations between citizens and governments is a major research area (Bertot et al. 2014; Ubaldi, 2013; Zuiderwijk and Janssen, 2014b). However, there is an argument that the e-government portal movement should give way to the open data movement (Robinson et al., 2009), turning control of data organization, presentation, and interpretation over to non-government entities, media, and interested citizens. Proponents argue that open data will lead to greater transparency, and hence to better oversight by citizens (Andersen, 2009; Bertot, Jaeger and Grimes, 2010a), greater civic participation (Francolli, 2011; Wahid, 2012), and more informed collaboration and debate (Ubaldi, 2013). McDermott (2010) outlines transparency, participation, and collaboration as the three hallmarks of open government (cf. Meijer, Curtin, and Hillebrandt, 2012).

A counterargument is that big data is too big and unorganized to be utilized effectively by anyone without significant digital tools and expertise and that big data is easily misinterpreted either intentionally or unintentionally. The most extreme form of this argument is that there is no such thing as "raw data" (Gitelman, 2013) and that all data has gone through some interpretive lens (Davies and Frank, 2013).

Open government and big data initiatives bump up against social media when we consider the possibility of "Social Government," or government and public services co-designed and co-produced by citizens and government entities (Bertot, Jaeger, and Grimes, 2010; Bertot, Jaeger, and Hanse, 2012; Bertot, Jaeger, Munson, and Glaisyer, 2010; Ferro et al., 2013; Mergel, 2013a; Scherer, Wimmer, and Strykowski, 2015). Attempts at designing social government systems, or at understanding how social government might be facilitated by social media platforms, identify several steps in co-production:

- identifying problems and needs;

- development of ideas;

- design of services for the public;

- implementation and diffusion of public services; and

- monitoring of public services.

Social government analysis recognizes that multiple stakeholders are involved in these steps, and social media can play the role of intermediary in bringing these stakeholders together. In this view, social media can be an enabler of crowdsourced problem solving involving citizens, government agencies, non-governmental organizations, and others (Chun et al., 2010; Doan, Ramakrishnan, and Halevy, 2011). Exploring inter-organizational collaboration using an open social media platform called WeChat that connects government entities, citizens, and university stakeholders, Wang, Medaglia, and Jensen (2016) found that collaboration was characterized by an ad-hoc and non-linear management of time, a sense of shared commitment to the accomplishment of tasks, serendipitous recruitment of team members based on expertise, and a transition from formal/professional to informal/private collaboration. This type of networked, collaborative government is recognized in the public administration literature as "New Public Service" (Brainard and McNutt, 2010), and is considered the most desirable way for government and citizens to interact (Bonsón et al., 2012; Grunig and Grunig, 2008).

Linders (2012) examines the impact of social technologies on the relationship between citizens and government. He notes that social media allows for the reemergence of "coproduction" whereby citizens are seen as partners in the development, implementation, and maintenance of government services. He explores three modes of coproduction:

- **Citizen Sourcing** (C2G), which involves citizens providing government with information to improve services;

- **Government as a Platform** (G2C) in which the government provides data and/or infrastructure on which citizens can build services;

- **Do It Yourself Government** (C2C) in which citizens band together to carry out or augment functions with which governments are traditionally tasked.

Linders further examines these modes of coproduction in the contexts of three stages of service delivery: design, execution, and monitoring. This allows for the analysis of systems into a 3×3 typology that crosses the modes of coproduction with the stages of service. For example, citizen-sourcing projects in the design phase might involve sharing citizen opinions with the government, as with eRulemaking systems. Citizen sourcing projects in the execution phase might involve crowdsourcing, as with challenge.gov where the government posts challenges and asks the public to propose solutions. Citizen sourcing projects in the monitoring phase might involve feedback from citizens about government services, as with various FixMyStreet applications that have appeared in many cities (King and Brown, 2007; Maeda, Sekimoto, and Seto, 2016).

2.4   SMART CITIES, "CIVIC TECH," AND URBAN INFORMATICS

At the current time, there is an emphasis on the concept of "smart cities." The smart cities movement is an attempt to take advantage of the information generated by multiple independent data-producing activities within an environment in order to understand otherwise invisible interconnected processes. Naphade et al. (2011) characterize a smart city as a "system of systems" in which interdependent public and private systems share information with each other, and with metasystems, to provide an integrated overview for purposes of planning, management, and operational efficiency. Smart cities often rely on data-generating sensors and monitors in addition to modeling and visualization software. For example, a traffic planner might utilize GPS data from phones in cars, camera data on highway density, weather data generated by multiple stations, social media text generated by commuters, and a myriad of other diverse information sets to generate a view of current traffic conditions, which might then be made available to users in visualizations of various kinds for multiple purposes.

The term "civic technology" (Civic Tech) has emerged to describe grass-roots, citizen-inspired technology development for civic purposes. Boehner and DiSalvo (2016) note that the field of human-computer interaction (HCI) has emphasized several aspects of the human side of computing technology in turn—including cognitive, followed by social, followed by cultural—and now may be turning to "civic."

Foth et al. (2015b) argue that civic engagement has finally become a critical issue for HCI for the following reasons.

- **Re-emergence of place:** There has been a move from the technology-enabled erosion of distance to place-based media and engagement.

- **Ubiquitous technology:** The integration of information technologies with every aspect of people's lives that have erased boundaries between the physical and digital city.

- **People as producers:** The ability for non-professionals to create content and design information systems encourages engagement that can have wide influence.

They specifically call out the technology trends of mobile/personal devices, broadband connectivity, open data, urban interfaces, and cloud computing as important in changing the outlook for civic engagement.

The Knight Foundation (Sotsky, 2013) identifies two overarching themes in civic tech: (1) Open Government; and (2) Community Action. Within each theme, several clusters were also described as follows:

- Open Government clusters:

    ○ Data Access and Transparency

    ○ Data Utility

    ○ Public Decision Making

    ○ Resident Feedback

    ○ Visualization and Mapping

    ○ Voting

- Community Action clusters:

    ○ Civic Crowdfunding

    ○ Community Organizing

    ○ Information Crowdsourcing

    ○ Neighborhood Forums

    ○ Peer-to-Peer Sharing

The Knight Foundation study found lower investment being placed in the Open Government clusters of voting, public decision-making, and resident feedback, and the Community Action cluster of civic crowdfunding. During the two-and-a-half-year study beginning in 2011, the most money was being invested in peer-to-peer sharing and neighborhood forum development, with this money coming primarily from private capital and not grant funding. Grant funding was supporting projects primarily in the data utility, data access and transparency, and resident feedback clusters.

More generally, Open Government initiatives were not supported by private investors, who instead preferred Community Action projects.

In reflecting on interviews with several civic tech innovators in the Atlanta area, Boehner and DiSalvo (2016) found that there was a move toward what they referred to as "Google-style" apps, or apps that emphasized search by information seekers instead of structure by information providers. This emphasis on supporting exploration instead of information design may have many implications for the flattening of governmental bureaucracies or procedures and the relationship between "data holders" and "data seekers."

The rise of urbanization and the concurrent spread of ubiquitous networked information technologies has given rise to a new area often called "urban informatics" (Foth, Choi, and Satchell, 2011). As the name implies, urban informatics deals with cities and has *place* as a central component of its professional identity, although place is considered both physically and digitally (Foth, 2009). Urban informatics as a discipline supports efforts to expose and utilize information to urban planners in addition to citizens who wish to influence and understand the environment in which they live and to engage with others in creating an urban community.

Foth (2017) distinguishes between "bird's-eye view" versus "street view" applications in the space of urban informatics. A bird's-eye view is a top-down approach often advocated by administrators in the service model of government in which digital government spaces are designed *for* citizens, whereas a street view is a community-centric approach empowering people to create their own urban spaces. The distinction is intended to emphasize citizens as active participants in creating civic space, and indeed to re-conceptualize the city as an interface environment between individuals and their physical spaces via ubiquitous computing (de Waal, 2014; Foth et al., 2015b).

2.5   HYPERLOCAL SOCIAL MEDIA

After the emergence of social media, development of community portals diminished precipitously. A collection of special purpose review and recommendation sites, for example restaurant review sites, took the place of the services sections of portals. Social media took the place of the discussion forums and bulletin boards that had been so carefully crafted, curated, and studied. This move, however, also resulted in a loss of the local, neighborhood-level quality of portals since service recommender and rating sites typically operate at a national or global level. Similarly, the most widely used social media platforms never implemented neighborhood-level, or even physical-space based networks, although it is possible to create them. Neighborhood-oriented social networks such as NextDoor have not seen the same kind of explosive adoption as sites like Yelp! in the recommender space, or Facebook in the social media space, or Twitter in the microblogging space have seen.

Nonetheless, some neighborhood and community networks have developed in the current digital environment. Known as "hyperlocal" social spaces, these can take multiple forms, including social media sites, Twitter handles, image sharing sites, and other forms. In contrast to the goals of many social media sites, hyperlocal social media is intended to be geographically bounded, connecting people who live together and presumably, therefore, have common concerns related to their neighborhood.

Masden et al. (2014) studied NextDoor, a relatively new, neighborhood-based social media environment currently deployed across the U.S. They contrast NextDoor with the earliest community network systems such as BEV, and note that it is one of the first nationwide, top-down efforts to support local social networking. BEV and other networks discussed at the beginning of this chapter all evolved from within their communities. They also point out that NextDoor finds a place in an already existing "civic media ecosystem" consisting of all other social media, and thus needs to provide affordances for a different type of local neighborhood experience. Their findings suggested that NextDoor was utilized by members of a community who already interacted more frequently than average. It was used along with other social media applications, however it was perceived as being more formal and serious than other social media and hence less prone to trolling and incivility. Because users are identified and live in proximity to each other, they did feel constrained in what they could post, citing concerns about privacy and trust. While the geographical boundaries did result in discussions of neighborhood issues, in contrast to other topics, they also hindered discussion of matters that concerned larger geographical areas (e.g., traffic).

Another approach to hyperlocal social media is to extract locally relevant information from social media feeds and present this filtered information to users. The goal of such systems, as with all community networks, is to create greater community awareness and involvement. However, in this approach the assumption is made that relevant local information is present in the larger stream of social media information and thus the goal is to find it and present it selectively to users within their communities. This has been a theme in several efforts, including LiveHoods to mine tweets and foursquare checkins as a way of modeling urban activity patterns (Cranshaw et al., 2012), CiVicinity for aggregating multiple social media sources (Carroll et al., 2015; Hoffman et al., 2012), Virtual Town Square (VTS) for local news aggregation (Kavanaugh et al., 2014), and Whoo.ly for extracting and summarizing local tweets (Hu, Farnham, and Monroy-Hernández, 2013).

The development of Whoo.ly provides a good example of how a hyperlocal system might be developed in a user-centered manner. The researchers first examined how community members use existing local information sources. They found that most community members are information consumers, not producers; that many people are local information pushers, usually via retweets; that some individuals become local information hubs and acquire many followers; and that people desire information passed along from other community members even when it is otherwise available through local news, blogs, and other sources. An examination of tweets relevant to local matters (in Seattle) revealed the following top ten categories in decreasing frequency:

- Neighborhood affirmations (bragging about the neighborhood)

- Business updates

- News

- Recommendations

- Civic activity

- Ads

- Social events

- Crime/Road reports

- Deals and coupons

- Talks and classes

This information allowed the designers to understand their potential users and the types of information that users would be hoping to see in a hyperlocal community tweet collection. Whoo.ly extracts local events, top local topics, active local people, and popular local places from Twitter and presents summaries to users in the relevant locality. An evaluation of Whoo.ly found that it was easier to use than the main Twitter feed and most useful to people who were not already skilled in Twitter filtering. They also found, however, that many users wished for more personalization and that providing all information about the locality was still something of an information overload issue.

CiVicinity (see Carroll et al., 2015 for an overview) provides another example of participatory development of a hyperlocal civic information aggregator. CiVicinity combined multiple sources of local information, including unusual sources such as electronic calendar entries and users' annotated photographs. The latter provide snapshots of smaller, more personal activities, which may enhance the sense of community engagement. The developers refer to this as "superthresholding," and compare it to small, neighborly acts such as commenting on the weather or showing someone a picture of a family member. The CiVicinity interface mixed maps, calendars, news, events, and stories. Formative evaluation showed that individuals found this integration of material provided a more comprehensive and cohesive information environment. There was some evidence that local news was perceived as being more important when presented in the community portal.

2.6   SUMMARY

We have traced the development of community networks from their inception, as listservs and portals designed and curated by community leaders; through the digital city metaphor; to the establishment of official e-government portals and services; to the smart city enabled by ubiquitous sensors and open data; and finally, to the rise of hyperlocal applications that mine the continuous and massive stream of user-generated and un-curated social media. While this reflects an evolution of technologies, it can also be seen as a change in the perception of what a digitally augmented community should be. Instead of being simply a provider of information and services, social media enabled the development of a community of discourse and, ultimately, a new definition of place.

CHAPTER 3

Theory

The advent of social media has relevance to theories of political discourse and political cognition. In this chapter, we examine several important theoretical positions about public discourse in civic situations in order to frame later discussion of research in this area. Relevant theory comes from many different traditions, including political science, media effects, sociology of self, and sociotechnical theories.

3.1 PUBLIC SPHERE

Perhaps the most important theoretical position for understanding social media and civic engagement is that of political philosopher Jürgen Habermas (1989) who is responsible for the term "public sphere," oft applied and reinterpreted in the context of social media. Habermas was heavily influenced by Hannah Arendt, who traced the evolution of the concepts of "public" and "private" spaces in the Western tradition from the time of Athenian democracy (esp. Arendt, 1958). According to Arendt's analysis, the ancient Greeks maintained a sense of the private sphere within the home relating to all matters of basic human necessity such as obtaining food and shelter and raising children.

Although every household had the same basic needs, these were not considered to be needs in common with others. These private needs were pursued independently by each household according to a strict hierarchical and patriarchal control structure. Indeed, what we now call the economy, the control of resources, was not a matter of common concern for the ancient Greeks, but existed as a private matter for each household unit. Members of a household or estate, who were considered property of the owner and included slaves, children, and women, did not concern themselves with matters beyond the private sphere and were quite invisible to each other across households and to the society at large. They engaged continuously and exclusively in what Arendt referred to as "labor," or day-to-day chores that maintained life but otherwise left no lasting artifacts or impressions.

By successfully developing a working household, the master of the house could then disengage with the necessities of life and begin to engage in more contemplative endeavors and the production of enduring works. Indeed, it was this collection of "free" men who met and formed the ancient Agora—a "public sphere" in the sense that the shared concerns of the Agora had nothing to do with the day-to-day needs of the various private spheres. This context nurtured the topics of the public sphere such as law, education, and relations among nation states; honed the skills of political participation such as rhetoric, logic, and persuasion; and produced enduring works such as buildings, legal canons, philosophical works, and epic stories.

A critical feature of the public sphere for Arendt was the need for a shared activity space in which citizens could meet to express their opinions and hear the perspectives of others. In fact, she maintained that political opinion could not occur in private and that it developed only from the characteristics of the public sphere. Citizens thus engaged develop a collective identity that is distinct from whatever private identities they might also have.

Developing from Arendt's ideas, Habermas notes that as the merchant class arose in 17th- and 18th-century Europe, it began to develop a social and political agenda that was separate from the ruling monarchies and noble classes. Members of these classes began to introduce previously private matters such as commerce into the public discourse. The economy left the realm of the private and became a public matter. Newspapers, pamphlets, and books began to carry political and economic news, and cafés and salons became natural meeting places for discussion of such issues. Habermas argued that this experience was the genesis of a sense of what he called the "bourgeois public sphere," a realm of discourse in which matters pertaining to the direction of the society could be discussed with the goal of actual implementation. The matter of political efficacy, the idea that civic and political discussion of non-elites could have actionable outcomes, is important since it is this sense of efficacy that makes the bourgeois public sphere a new and unique concept and that ultimately enabled the development of democratic governance. Habermas claims that this period saw the emergence of what has come to be called "public opinion," or a set of attitudes and beliefs derived from civic discourse and available to a larger citizenry. Public opinion developed in such contexts was often critical of state policies and had the aim of changing them.

Habermas further argued that prior to the emergence of the bourgeois public sphere, nobles considered themselves to be the state, and other people were subjects of the state. After the development of the public sphere, the concept underwent a change such that individuals came to think of themselves as constituting the state through their multitude of private interests. Private interests were then expressed through "representation" of the private at the level of the state, eventually through representative governance models of various kinds.

Many scholars have attempted to distill the essential characteristics of the public sphere (Dahlberg, 2004; Dean, 2003). Most enduring has been Dahlberg's six "idealizing presuppositions," or essential qualities that must be present for a public sphere to operate.

- **Reasoned exchange of problematic validity claims.** Argument is at the core of the public sphere and argument implies the existence of competing claims about what is true. The ability to make such claims publicly, identify their coexistence as problematic, and begin discourse about them is a critical presupposition. This conceptualization of the public sphere posits universal solutions and non-contextualized truth assumptions.

- **Reflexivity.** The ability to examine one's own values and beliefs is essential to productive discourse.

- **Ideal role taking.** The ability to understand the perspective of another with the goal of ultimate agreement.

- **Sincerity.** Rational discourse toward a productive end requires that the participants actually intend to reach consensus. This precludes modes of discourse aimed as misleading others.

- **Formal inclusion and discursive equality.** Equality of participation is critical if all points of view are to be heard, reflected in the discourse, and constitutive of the outcome. Habermas recognized that this must be realized not just formally, but in actual practice through the elimination of barriers to participation such as social class, language, status, and so on.

- **Autonomy from state and corporate power.** Even though discourse within the public sphere impacts the governments, corporations, and other power structures within the culture, these institutions must not influence discourse within the public sphere.

In the 20th century, Habermas claims that mass consumerism and the rise of global capitalism have overwhelmed the public sphere with commercial interests aimed at largely private affairs. In modern society, the economic interests of corporations and commercial enterprises have come to dominate public discourse, which is now filled with attempts to influence citizens' perceptions of their basic needs and direct their actions to further the economic interests of others. Many contemporary observers of the internet note that virtual public spaces are almost all commercial ventures at their core, raising the question of how much this influences the types of discourse possible within virtual public spheres.

Habermas' concept of the public sphere has been criticized on several counts, the most important for our purposes being that it presupposes and privileges a critical/rational style of argumentation that is not universal and may, in fact, be both counterproductive and exclusionary. The other is that the pubic spheres that Habermas describes are highly selective in terms of who is actually welcome (e.g., gender and class distinctions) and equipped to participate (Fraser, 1990; McLaughlin, 2004). Habermas (2004) himself noted that the advent of one-way mass communication technology (i.e., television) has "refeudalised" the public sphere and greatly increased the influence of commercialism in controlling messaging. Finally, the concept of the public sphere is largely built on analyses of Western societies, although Wang's (2008) study of Chinese teahouses in early- and mid-20th century Sichuan Province suggests that the ideas may generalize culturally.

The theory of the public sphere was developed and grew before the internet. Of course, with the advent of the internet and its uptake by a broader public, the question of whether and how the public sphere might be realized in virtual space emerged. Dahlgren (2005) further analyses the public sphere as it is formed via the internet, a process which he refers to as the "cyber transformation of the public sphere" (p. 151). He observes that we should now consider that there are multiple public spheres and that they offer differing possibilities for engagement. This *sprawling* nature of the public sphere comes about because citizens use multiple social and new media tools to communicate with each other and learn about civic issues. One criticism of research on the digital public sphere is that researchers tend to focus on and generalize from single application contexts without recognizing that users are typically in many application contexts.

Dahlgren (2005) distinguishes among structural, representational, and interactional dimensions of public spheres.

- **The structural dimension** in the context of the internet involves all "legal, social, economic, cultural, technical, and … architectural features" (p. 149). This is interesting in terms of the notion of *affordance*, which will be treated in a later chapter. Structural aspects of the public sphere are those which enable public discourse and include not just institutions (e.g., traditional media, social media applications) but also the policies and practices of those institutions as they impact free and unfettered discourse.

- **Representational aspects of the public sphere** involve the output or product(s) of media, social media, and other institutions. The success of a public sphere can be judged by the preferred characteristics of output, such as "fairness, accuracy, completeness, pluralism of views, agenda setting, ideological tendencies, modes of address" (p. 149).

- **Interactional aspects of a public sphere** involve the actors', both human and institutional, interactions with each other—their nature, directionality, and so forth.

Dahlgren (2005, 2009) builds on Habermas's vision by introducing the concept of civic culture. He contends that there exist six preconditions of mutual reciprocity for participation in the public sphere, including: knowledge, values, trust, spaces, practices, and identities. When one of these conditions is not met, people's ability to participate can be inhibited.

- **Knowledge and competence** refers to the idea that a citizens' ability to participate in the public sphere requires that they be able to acquire and disseminate knowledge. When discussing this capability, Dahlgren notes that there are multiple, fragmented public spheres each of which may encapsulate knowledge and require different competencies for participation. This is potentially problematic for democracy to the degree that citizens have difficulty navigating multiple public spheres.

- **Values** refer to a citizens' ability to engage in the public sphere as dictated by the values of openness, reciprocity, discussion, and accountability.

- **Affinity and Trust** refer to the idea that some commonalities must exist among individuals despite the heterogeneous nature of modern culture. Individuals must be able to adequately engage with people they may or may not know personally, but feel that they can have a satisfactory exchange.

- **Spaces** (offline and online) through which people can meet and discuss political candidates and issues.

- **Practices** refer to the activities people engage in, both individually and collectively, to participate in the public sphere. They include practices clearly related to democracy, such as voting, and other practices in which culture is experienced and shared, such as television watching or social media browsing.

- **Identities** involve the concept that people have an awareness of the characteristics that comprise their political beliefs and attitudes, and that they have the right to those attitudes and beliefs.

Zizi Papacharissi has contributed significantly to theory about the public sphere in the context of new media and social media (Papacharissi, 2009, 2012). Papacharissi (2012) notes that there are three aspects of internet-enabled public sphere applications with which researchers and theorists concern themselves: access to information, reciprocity of communication, and commercialization of online space.

Papacharissi notes that the "virtual sphere 2.0" offers several modifications to the public sphere, the most interesting ones being *personalization* and *agonistic pluralism*. Personalization involves organizing streams of information in a way that reflects self-interest and self-concept. It also involves sharing private information that is not only opinion-related, but also related to self-expression. Papacharissi claims that this mode of making the private public has emerged in postmodern society that places value on self-expression and what she terms "civically motivated narcissism" (p. 237). She finds that blogs, video logs, and other self-centered narrative internet forms are often expressions of autonomy and can be used to question authority and assert control over the political environment. Hence, they have played a powerful role in subversive civic movements and collective action. She further notes that blogs and self-expressive media can "challenge the established public agenda in an anarchic manner" (p. 238) and bring more diverse viewpoints into the public discourse, although she also argues that these outlets play a small role enhancing democracy and energizing a true public sphere as it was originally conceptualized.

The possibility of more direct representation on the internet and within social media has been enthusiastically described by several theorists and researchers. Papacharissi (2004) observes, however, that discourse in such virtual spaces is often antagonistic and diverse, which is not technically consistent with the traditional notion of the public sphere. Citing Mouffe (2000), she claims that citizens are often confused about what is happening in a diverse and abrasive discourse environment and how exactly it is a form of democratic dialogue. Mouffe (2000) notes that there must be some common ground among individuals in order to foster productive democratic discourse. That said, it is possible for a group of citizens who disagree to share a coherent sense of purpose *vis a vis* particular problems and issues and to engage in "agonistic" discourse concerning these issues (Mouffe, 2005). Agonistic discourse is distinguished from antagonistic discourse in that there is an attempt by participants and observers to learn from disagreement. As such, "agonistic pluralism" (Mouffe, 2005; Papacharissi, 2009), or the expression of multiple points of view, arises again as a foil to existing power structures that would otherwise constrain discourse by, in this case, insisting on coherence of perspectives.

Papacharissi (2004) found that political discourse in newsgroups was often heated, but not necessarily impolite or "uncivil." The distinction involves issue disagreement and emotionally charged expression (heated) on the one hand, versus conversational and social norm violation (impoliteness) and personal antagonism (incivility) on the other. She relates her observations to Lyotard (1984) and Schudson (1997), who stressed that disagreement and anarchy can be healthy for progressive democratic purposes, and to Poster (1997), who argues that fluid identities online lead to difficulty in forming consensus but also to greater expression of diverse viewpoints and hence more democratic discourse.

The sprawling nature of the public sphere and the multiple technologies currently available for social interaction create an environment in which multiple interests converge. Convergence of multiple spheres means that entertainment, politics, culture, friendship, and other matters are often encountered together. The notion of *third spaces* (Oldenburg, 1999) has arisen to describe non-work and non-home environments that allow for a multiplicity of discourses to take place, and naturally the idea has been expanded to include virtual third spaces, including social media and other virtual spaces with social components such as online games, MOOCs, etc. (Rheingold, 2002; Soukup, 2006).

Several researchers have begun to explore how the new landscape of technologically mediated political discourse might change the very ideas of democracy and participation. Theory along these lines stresses several novel qualities of contemporary political dialog, including the fact that it is global, ubiquitous, heterogeneous, and confrontational. Many post-public sphere theorists note that the future of the public sphere will be ever more fragmented, completely separated from geography (e.g., cities, nations), and with little distinction between private and public.

In a prominent critique of the public sphere notion, Dean (2003) proposes that we think about new types of democratic discourse ("neodemocracies") and states that "[r]eimagining democracy under conditions of global technoculture is a project that is just beginning" (Dean, 2003 p 111). According to Dean, instead of considering that the web creates a public sphere that enables a global deliberative discourse, we should consider that the web has instead allowed for the formation of multiple "democratic configurations" of individuals. These configurations contrast with the ideal of the public sphere in several ways.

- **Non-geopolitical spaces:** The public sphere was usually conceptualized as being associated with a political state such as a nation or a city, but neodemocratic institutions may be more dispersed, and multiple institutions might exist in the same place.

- **Contestation:** Consensus was a hallmark goal of the public sphere, but the existence and description of important differences characterizes much of technologically mediated political discourse and may, in itself, be an ideal of such discourse. In fact, this suggests that the design of technological discourse systems might need to support conflict transparency as much as consensus building.

- **Duration instead of inclusivity:** The goal of much social and new media is to engage and maintain attention, which often means shifting agendas and stories with frequency. The ability to maintain focus on a particular issue over an extended period of time thus becomes a new goal of neodemocratic systems. Dean argues that this replaces the inclusivity goal of the public sphere because (a) true inclusivity has never been practical anyway, and (b) inclusivity is irrelevant if the public cannot maintain attention on the issue.

- **Hegemony instead of equality:** The goal of hearing and weighing all sides has had as its ideal outcome that an agreement will be reached that somehow melds all perspectives, beliefs, and viewpoints in a common solution. A different approach is to accept that there is no compromise in some political disputes, especially those that are rooted in deep beliefs and senses of identity (e.g., LGBTQ issues, women's rights). This view replaces the Habermasian ideal of equality with one in which there are clear winners and losers. The goal of political discourse in a neodemocratic context, then, is to essentially win over as many people as possible to one side of an argument, hence hegemony replaces equality in this point of view.

- **Decisiveness instead of transparency:** Dean argues that the ideal of transparency, or making clear and visible the motivations and actions of others, may actually weaken democratic deliberation in the contemporary era of information glut. Thus, deliberation aimed at making decisions and motivating action is emphasized.

- **Credibility over rationality:** Finally, the idea that there is a universal form of rational discourse and rational decision making, one in which all people would ultimately agree, is questioned. The notion of credibility suggests that neodemocratic discourse will recognize that there are different ways of knowing and that credibility to persons and ideas may be assigned differentially by different interest groups.

Dahlberg (2011) outlines "positions" on how digital democracy might be realized. His analysis allows for consensus forms of deliberation, more confrontational forms of argument, and alternative collaboration and sharing activities. The positions, and the digital affordances that each provides are as follows.

- **Liberal-consumer:** A competitive/aggregative conception of democracy. Digital affordances include articulating, associating, campaigning, contesting, forming groups, identifying, organizing, protesting, resisting.

- **Deliberative:** A deliberative/consensual conception of democracy. Digital affordances include agreeing, arguing, deliberating, disagreeing, informing, meeting, opinion forming, publicizing, reflecting

- **Counter-publics:** A "contestationary" conception of democracy. Digital affordances include articulating, associating, campaigning, contesting, forming groups, identifying, organizing, protesting, resisting.

- **Autonomous Marxist:** A commons/networking conception of democracy. Digital affordances include collaborating, cooperating, distributing, exchanging, giving, networking, participating, sharing.

When taking a *liberal-consumer* point of view, citizens' relationship to government is one of rights and claims. Citizens are often in conflict with each other but each will act in his or her own best interest to learn about and gain what they need for themselves. Their decisions are based on rational reflection about their own needs and depend on gaining information and expressing themselves through mechanisms like voting.

When taking a *deliberative* point of view, citizens try to understand each other and strive to develop solutions that are mutually acceptable. Their decisions are based on hearing and taking the perspectives of others and acting by persuasion and the creation of a larger "public opinion." The deliberative perspective is most closely aligned with the ideal of the public sphere.

When taking a *counter-publics* point of view, citizens strive to identify groups with which they have commonalities and differences. Their actions involve the strengthening of their group(s) in contrast with others and identifying to contrasting publics what their differences are. The counter-public perspective is most closely aligned with Papacharissi's agonistic pluralism and Dean's neodemocracies.

Finally, the *autonomous Marxist* point of view derives from a countercultural, anti-authoritarian tradition that rejects hierarchy and emphasizes the ability of individuals to resist power structures without recourse to alternative organizational entities such as political parties, labor unions, and so on (Cuninghame, 2010; Hardt and Negri, 2000). Their actions are anti-establishment activities such as formation of sharing collectives, popup demonstrations (e.g., the Occupy movement), and viral protest. In this perspective, ultimately a "multitude of singularities," or a collective with common interests, takes control of the commons, and society is capable of running itself in something akin to a swarm intelligence in a mode similar to the way Wikipedia or IndyMedia operate (see Nothhaft, 2016). This latter perspective on digital democracy is a form of "cyber-libertarianism," described by Dahlberg (2010) as follows:

> *"The cyber-libertarian 2.0 discourse celebrates the technologically enabled autonomy and resourcefulness of a liberal-individualist DIY citizen-consumer whose digital networking is understood to constitute an egalitarian, conflict free realm transcending existing political institutions – that is, to constitute a libertarian 'Web 2.0 democracy'"* (p. 348).

However, Dahlberg critiques this perspective by offering some limits. Thus, Dahlgren's view of autonomous Marxism includes participatory and cooperative sharing activities that the most extreme forms of cyber-libertarianism do not.

In a similar attempt to characterize multiple types of political discourse in digital forums, Freelon (2010) expands upon many of the public sphere models of democratic communication. In addition to the *deliberative* style that favors rational argument, equality, reciprocity, and discussion across ideological boundaries, Freelon (2010) describes *liberal individualist* and *communitarian* forms of deliberative communication. Communitarian modes of discourse stress social cohesion and formation of group identity. Dialog in this mode is ideologically homophilous, often has a goal of mobilization, stresses identity, and has considerable within-ideology questioning and response. Liberal individualist modes of discourse are characterized by self-expression. Examples of dialog in this mode are flaming, personal revelation and self-promotion, and monologue.

3.2   SOCIAL CAPITAL AND CIVIL SOCIETY

The concept of *social capital* is invoked to explain why people come together in collective organizations and friend/acquaintance networks to achieve ends that they might not otherwise be able to achieve as individuals. The term "capital" is used to indicate that membership in social groups imparts resource advantages of various kinds to members and can allow them to achieve both collective and individual goals more easily than non-members. Coleman (1988, 1990) made an early attempt to define a type of human capital that could be characterized by relationships and bonds that are formed for instrumental purposes. His quest was to link sociology and economics, or more grandly to link models of social action with the rational actor models of economics. Coleman claimed that social capital, unlike other forms of human capital, is not found or held by individuals but rather is an emergent property of the structural relations among actors. This means that it can dissipate and its value can become null to individuals if the social structure from which it arises breaks down.

As Foley and Edwards (1997) point out, Coleman found social capital to have no intrinsic value beyond what individuals could achieve, and in fact Coleman describes both positive and negative effects to society from the formation of social groups that accrue value for themselves. Coleman's view is thus highly structural and his analyses focus on the utilitarian aspects of context-specific and goal-driven social relationships. Coleman finds that social networks can be formed and held together based on matters of trust, expectation, norms, obligation, and authority. Some of these mechanisms may have positive social value, others negative social value, and others neutral social value.

Putnam (1995) reinvigorated discussion of social capital by aligning it with positive social value and asserting that its decline in modern society was leading to an erosion of civic institutions and the values to society that they imbue. Putnam's argument rests on the assumption that social capital depends primarily on reciprocity and trust in others, which in turn has positive virtues in the larger civic sphere. In fact, Putnam, like Tocqueville (1969), went so far as to argue that the health of civil society itself could be measured in terms of the social capital generated and nurtured by the polity.

Considerable research on social capital involves the examination of the nature of ties between individuals in a network (Lin, 2001, 2008). One important characteristic of social networks is the strength of ties, which have been quantified in many ways. In a classic paper, Granovetter (1973, 1982) distinguished between strong and weak ties (defined in this case as frequency of contact and number of common ties) and found that weak ties were often more important than strong ties as sources of useful information for activities such as finding new jobs. Granovetter explained this phenomenon by noting that weak ties connect otherwise disparate parts of a larger set of networks and that connections made across weak ties therefore contribute to social cohesion at a macroscopic level of analysis, in other words at a level of analysis that includes the connections among communities as well as connections among individuals within those communities.

Thus began a line of research on social capital that examines both the external structure of relations among groups of actors ("bridging" social capital) and the internal ties that bind members of groups ("bonding" social capital). Needless to say, the advent of computer-mediated social networks has revived social network analysis and, with it, theories of social capital and analysis of the human attitudes that drive sociability. At the same time, the possibility of utilizing social networks for e-government and civic engagement has also resulted in the re-emergence of discussions of the health of democratic institutions and their reliance on social coherence, trust, reciprocity and other civic values (Adler and Kwon 2002).

3.3   NETWORKED SELF AND CONTEXT COLLAPSE

Political participation involves individuals presenting themselves vis-à-vis a political issue or candidate. In the simplest form this means declaring that one is pro or con. In a more complex form this involves arguing for a position and defending oneself against others with differing opinions. In any form, with the exception of casting a secret ballot, political participation is an act of self-disclosure. In the context of social media, this self-disclosing activity extends to the consumption and production of news. In social media, the fact that someone has looked at a news article or opinion piece, and certainly the fact that somebody likes/recommends this content, is widely broadcast. Hence, theories of presentation of self are also often invoked in the research literature on online participation.

Goffman (1990) grounds most theories of the self as a presentational phenomenon that is actively created by individuals in social contexts and co-constructed by interaction with others. Goffman's analysis made sociology as critical to theories of self as psychology had been previously. With the advent of ICTs and, especially social media, social and presentational theories of the self have been used to understand behavior within these media (Hogan, 2010).

One result of the development of the internet has been an increased emphasis on networked individuals. Several researchers (boyd, 2010; Castells, 2001; Papacharissi, 2012; Wellman, 2001) describe the "networked self" and how it is manifest via new media, social media, and internet discourse in general. In modern society, the performative aspect of self may be more significant than ever before (Madison and Hamera, 2006). Due to the reach of social networks and other networking technologies like microblogs, the network formed by an individual's connections is far broader than in the past—no longer constrained by geographical or sociocultural boundaries. This at once results in a release from nationalism and parochialism as important components of networked identity while enabling a more globalized sense of identity and, hence, activism.

Networked theories of the self shift attention to the audience or, more accurately, the *imagined audience* (boyd, 2008; Brake, 2012; Litt, 2012; Marwick and boyd, 2011; Semaan et al., 2015) of social media activity. Individuals are acutely aware that their activities on the internet are public to varying degrees and this awareness guides their choices, both as producers and consumers of information. Social media users present themselves to others via an ongoing process of what Papacharissi and Easton (2012) identify as authorship, listening, and redaction.

Social media is a conversation, and as such is dialogical, or dependent on participants' considerations about their presentation of self and what others think of them. While the notion of "dialogical self," or a perception of the self as derived from interactions with others and as mutable depending on the perceived audience, has lengthy history (Hermans and Kempen, 1993), even including William James's theory of the "social self" (Cooper, 1992; James 1890), the reach of social media has made the issue of imagined audience much more complex for individuals and thus richer for theorists (boyd, 2010; Brake, 2012; Marwick and boyd, 2014; Papacharissi, 2013). Digital natives who have come of age in the internet era and who have used social media in their formative years may in fact have a greater sense of audience, a more fluid self-image, and a more faceted identify (Cook and Teasley, 2011; Farnham and Churchill, 2011; Litt and Hargittai, 2016).

In a study of Facebook, Twitter, and LinkedIn users, Litt and Hargittai (2016) found that people were highly fluid in their sense of the imagined audience and that they maintained many categories of audiences. About half the time, social media users' messages were thought of as going to an "abstract imagined audience" (or no one in particular). Half of their posts, however, had targets that fell into the following categories.

- **Personal ties:** Family members and good friends.

- **Communal ties:** Acquaintances who were known to the posters because of shared interests, memberships in groups, common locations (neighbors), and shared experiences.

- **Professional ties:** People the posters knew or had met at work, in school, and in other formal situations.

- **Phantasmal ties:** People with whom the posters imagined a connection, such as celebrities, politicians, and deceased individuals. This category also includes non-human audiences such as companies and organizations.

People using social media sometimes have an audience in mind for each individual post, but they often have only a vague sense of who might be interested in what they are saying. Litt and Hargittai (2016) suggest that an abstract audience may be the default for many social media users. The lack of a concept of who one is addressing, possibly because of the cognitive difficulty in making such a determination, is referred to as "context collapse" (Marwick and boyd, 2014; Vitak, 2012), consequential because of its implications for how social media users negotiate their discourse, understand its impact, and reflect on themselves. The development of tools and strategies for selecting audiences and managing context collapse is an important area of research (Vitak et al., 2012).

3.4   USES AND GRATIFICATIONS

Uses and Gratifications (U&G) is a theoretical framework that arose in the context of media studies (Katz, 1959; Katz, Blumler and Gurevitch, 1973; Rubin, 1993) and has been applied more recently to the use of social media in many contexts (Joinson, 2008), including political and civic contexts (Papacharissi and Mendelson, 2011; Papacharissi and Rubin, 2000). The original goal of U&G theory was to explain why individuals choose certain media and reject others. U&G theory shifts the focus of media studies from effects of media to choices and actions of media users (Katz, 1959; Parker and Plank, 2000; Rubin, 2002; Ruggiero, 2000).

Ruggiero (2000) criticized U&G in the context of new media on the grounds that it focuses too heavily on the individual and thereby minimizes related social and cultural matters. However, with the advent of social media, the motivations for choices by information consumers have become even more important, since social media browsing is a highly active process driven by a series of user choices made in continuously changing contexts which include social contexts and motivations (Ancu and Cozma, 2009).

Katz, Gurevitch, and Haas (1973) identified five needs related to the consumption of media in general:

- cognitive needs related to knowledge and information;

- affective needs related to emotional experience;

- personal/self-integrative needs related to confidence;

- social-integrative needs related to social capital and social networks; and

- escapism or tension-release needs.

Studies of U&G for social media (Park, Kee, and Valenzuela, 2009b; LaRose and Eastin, 2004) tend to find similar needs:

- socializing;

- entertainment;

- self-status seeking; and

- information.

Ancu and Cozmo (2009) found that three of the above needs—socializing, entertainment, and information seeking—provide the bulk of explanation for why people visit political social media sites. Gil de Zúñiga, Valenzuela, and Weeks (2016) used structural equation modeling to un-cover a set of civic-oriented and social-oriented motivations for engaging in political discussion on social media. The "citizen-communication model" says that media is used for information purposes, which is then used to feed interpersonal discussion. Discussion in turn exposes people to new ideas and resources and thus becomes a vector to civic action (Lee, Shah, and McLeod, 2013; Shah et al., 2005). Online media seems to have a stronger influence on this chain of causality because of its easy transition between the informational and the social (Lee, Shah, and McLeod, 2013). Social media also allows people to be producers of information, and evidence suggests that civic engagement is also positively associated with online production (Bakker and de Vreese, 2011; Östman, 2012; Quintelier and Vissers, 2008).

Ekström and Östman (2013) claim that adolescents have four primary dimensions that motivate their use of the internet:

- informational;

- interactional;

- expressive; and

- recreational.

The first three are most important for civic engagement. They found that internet use for information gathering purposes was not a predictor of factual political knowledge (in contrast to the use of more traditional media) but that it was a predictor of offline political engagement in the form of discussions with peers and family. Information gathering, online interaction, and frequency of creative internet use (contributing to blogs, for example) were predictors of online and offline political deliberation and action.

Naturally, maintaining social connections is the most important need satisfied by social media, and it includes both online and offline networks (Ellison, Steinfield, and Lampe, 2007). Entertainment has become a more important need fulfilled by social media as SNSs have integrated video (e.g., the Facebook-YouTube mashup) and text has become less prominent (Haridakis and Hanson, 2009). The presentation of self is an important factor in SNS use and has studied extensively in its own right (Tufekci, 2008; Walther et al., 2008).

The information need is highly relevant to use of SNSs in politics and civic engagement (Papacharissi and Rubin, 2000). Political and civic issues always show up as important categories of information sought by SNS users (Ancu and Cozma, 2009; Park, Kee, and Valenzuela, 2009b), although many SNS users also like to engage directly with candidates, fulfilling a social need as well (Ancu and Cozma, 2009). Although this motivation is common, engagement with politics is not a major factor in SNS use (Mihailidis, 2014).

In the context of SNSs, the question might be applied to why people choose different platforms (Semaan et al., 2015), why they dwell on certain posts and not on others, and why they choose to read or contribute.

3.5   AGENDA SETTING AND FRAMING

Agenda setting is a phenomenon related to uses and gratifications but more focused on media effects than on personal goals. Media effects is a broad category of theories concerning how mass media influences attitudes, beliefs, and actions. A major way that mass media influences the public is by creating a sense of what topics are interesting at the moment, usually by sustained focus on those topics over time and across media outlets, giving rise to a sense of "public opinion." McCombs and Shaw (1972) first documented the fact that sustained media attention to certain topics resulted in the belief by voters that these topics were the most important in determining which candidate to choose. They coined the term "agenda setting" to describe how media attention created a sense of salience about certain issues which in turn correlated with their perceived importance (Kiousis, 2004; Roberts, Wanta, and Dzwo, 2002).

In addition to creating a sense of what topics are most important, agenda setting can influence what characteristics a citizen believes are important or salient about a politician or other public figure. In agenda-setting theory, greater attention to a topic or to characteristics of a person leads to a "stronger attitude" about that topic or those characteristics (Kiousis and McCombs, 2004). Salient issues and characteristics then take on greater power in influencing opinions. Media effects, which are external to citizens, can be seen as contrasting with a pure Uses and Gratifications model in which citizens pay attention to issues that have significance based on internal factors. Agenda setting and the concepts of public opinion and public attention have since been studied extensively (Bryant and Miron, 2004; McCombs and Shaw, 1993; McCombs, 2014; Wanta and Ghanem, 2007).

Agenda-setting theories initially focused on the amount of coverage given to topics by media. Subsequent theory has investigated how the types of coverage might influence attitudes and opinions (Weaver, 2007). The manner in which different messages influence opinions and attitudes is often referred to in media effects studies as "framing" (Chong and Druckman, 2007). An important aspect of framing is how exciting or dramatic the issue frame is. More dramatic issue framing leads to greater interest and to greater influence of a news item (Wanta and Hu, 1993). Another important aspect of framing involves the degree of knowledge that individuals possess about a topic. Agenda setting is more likely for issues that are not well known or understood (Smith, 1987), with more abstract issues in contract to concrete matters (Yagade and Dozier, 1990).

The expansion of agenda-setting theory into the world of social media is a type of "intermedia effect." The study of intermedia effects is concerned with the shared agenda-setting role of multiple news outlets, especially across media platforms, as when a newspaper story spurs attention by television news, for example. Intermedia effects tend to flow from mainstream sources to less-reputable or less well-known media entities (Lim, 2006).

A considerable literature has grown recently on the role of the web in agenda setting (Neuman et al., 2014; Parmelee, 2013; Wallsten, 2007). Several studies of online media have similarly shown that agenda setting flows from online traditional media to more citizen-centric blogs and bulletin boards (Ceron, Curini, and Iracus, 2016; Cornfield et al., 2005; Meraz, 2009; Vargo, Basilaia and Shaw, 2015; Roberts, Wanta, and Dzwo, 2002). As social networks have evolved, however, citizen-to-citizen news flow has increased dramatically (Ceron, 2015; Meraz, 2011; Meraz and Papacharissi, 2013), and some researchers argue that major news is now beginning to pick up information from non-professional online sources such as blogs and social media sites (Conway, Kenski and Wang, 2015; Lloyd, Kaulgud, and Skiena, 2006; Parmelee, 2013; Wallsten, 2010; Woodly, 2008).

3.6   STRUCTURATION

Structuration theory is a way of understanding systems that gives equal weight to the agents (groups of people) involved in forming a system and the structure of the system itself (Giddens, 1984). According to structuration theory, social structures are at once produced by actors while at the same time providing a medium within which actors are bounded in their thoughts, feelings, and behaviors. This *duality of structure* thesis guides analysis of human activity. Adaptive Structuration Theory (DeSanctis and Poole, 1994) is a further iteration of the theory that deemphasizes technology constraints and seeks to understand how technology is dynamically reimagined and repurposed by users. This approach is especially useful in understanding communication-enabling technologies with purposes such as social media.

Carpentier (2011, 2015) distinguishes among access, interaction, and participation. Access to information is achieved when people and organizations are present to create and consume content. Mass communication technologies enable people to have *access* to a large amount of information, and people's information consumption choices provide feedback to media companies about what is desired. Social technologies allow organizations and people to co-create content and enable people to *interact* with others in the context of such content and within the constraints of the media platforms. Truly *participatory* technologies would allow for people and organizations to share power in terms of content creation, agenda setting, organizational policies and even platform design. For example, when considering political debates, mass media allowed people to watch as an audience an event that the media had organized. People watching a debate in a mass media context have no power to structure the debate. The integration of social technologies into debate coverage allowed not only the ability for some audience members to interact with the event (via moderators reading Tweets to the candidates, for example), but also allowed for widespread interaction among citizens during the debates. Finally, a truly participatory debate would allow for the audience to share control of the action, or even take control of the action, with moderators playing a more minor role. The latter has not truly been achieved.

Macek (2015) has examined these aspects of structuration theory in the context of social and new media. Social media and mobile platforms have erased the previously distinct spaces in which the public versus private distinction is made. Macek calls the current state of affairs "diffused participation" and relates it to Abercrombie and Longhurst's (1998) concept of "diffused audience," the idea that we have now become at once performers and audience in a more explicit and sensational manner than sociologists in the dramaturgical tradition (Goffman, 1990) could ever have imagined.

Mass media set cultural agendas that could be shared by multiple individuals and brought the public sphere into the private space of people's living rooms. Ubiquitous and social media, on the other hand, deconstructs the mass and empowers individuals to structure the experiences of others in their networked spheres ("private publics") on the one hand, and to serve as audiences for their networked friends on the other. Thus, performance theory and imagined audience become important lenses through which to understand the experience of civic participation in the new media age.

ICT research in this tradition examines how people create structures that are realized in technology design and how these structures and artifacts, in turn, come to define what people do and how they view their activities (Macek, 2013; Stones, 2005).

3.7   ACTOR-NETWORK THEORY

Actor-Network Theory (ANT) has been adopted from sociology as an alternative view to the idea that "social" is a special state of affairs that carries some explanatory power (Latour, 2005). A significant aspect of ANT for sociotechnical systems researchers is that ANT makes no distinction between human and non-human (usually technical) actors who work together toward an end. Instead, ANT as a theory and as a method proposes that heterogeneous agents form "assemblages" that may be construed as an actor, without further deconstruction, in analysis of activities and behaviors. Research in this area typically is aimed at understanding how "assemblages" come together (and possibly come apart) and then how they act together as a system. ANT analyses are often highly descriptive and a-theoretical.

In political science and social media studies, the ANT perspective is often employed as a counter to the tendency to describe social groups as actors, e.g., liberals and conservatives, voters and non-voters, etc. According to ANT, this privileges the agency of humans and ignores the larger sociotechnical structures in which their actions take place.

As far as social media and politics are concerned, an analysis of a political movement like Occupy (Beraldo and Galan-Paez, 2013) would take the people involved, the devices and services they are using, and the social media networks formed as an entity to be analyzed as a whole, de-emphasizing differences in organizational and individual perspectives. Using ANT as an analytical lens, it would be inappropriate to just look at whether a new technology had a particular effect, for example whether a mobile social app would increase civic participation. Instead, the appropriate analysis would be to explore the new actor-networks (people, organizations, and technological artifacts) that formed in co-construction with the technology.

3.8   INFORMATION DIFFUSION

Information diffusion theory developed as a way to understand how information flows through a network and what factors facilitate and hinder information diffusion. Theories are usually linked back to classic *diffusion of innovation* studies (Rogers, 1995; Strang and Soule, 1998), but in the context of social media, the emphasis is on why particular messages, images, memes, news items, or other content are shared and how they spread among friends, weak ties, groups, etc. (Cosley et al., 2010; Gruhl et al., 2004; Leskovec, Adamic, and Huberman, 2007a; Leskovec et al., 2007b; Sun et al., 2009). The spread of information through networks is a function of influence and homophily (Aral, Muchnik, Sundararajan, 2009; Kossinets and Watts, 2009).

In a simulation study, Romero, Meeder, and Kleinberg (2011b) found that political hashtags on Twitter travel more extensively than many other types of hashtags such as sports or celebrities. Other researchers have found that news sources travel more quickly than blog sources (Leskovec, Backstrom, and Kleinberg, 2009), and that unexpected information travels more quickly than expected information (Crane and Sornette, 2008). Suh et al. (2010) discuss the idea that users of Twitter calculate the value of information from multiple factors, including contact factors, such as whether a tweet contains a hashtag or URLs and popularity characteristics of the person who originated the tweet, as measured by the number of followers and retweet count.

Two common measures of information diffusion in Twitter are *stickiness* and *persistence* (Romero, Meeder, and Kleinberg, 2011b). Stickiness is the probability that a piece of information will be retweeted after first contact, and persistence is the likelihood of continuing retweeting. Thus, stickiness and persistence are measures of how quickly and thoroughly information spreads through a network.

Information brokers, or individuals who play the role of disseminating significant information to many others, have been identified in social networks (van Liere, 2010). Romero et al. (2011a) have described an algorithm to determine both the influence and passivity of users based on their retweet profiles, arguing that it is not enough to be influential (i.e., popular), but successful information brokers must also have ways to overcome user passivity.

Starbird and Palen (2010, 2012) identified information brokers among Twitter users during crisis situations and documented their importance in organizing actionable tweets for others. They point out that information diffusion in crisis situations is a kind of crowd work that helps to filter and focus messaging (as opposed to adding noise to a signal).

3.9   SUMMARY

There are many theories relevant both to the use of social media and to the activities involved in civic engagement. However, the ones presented in this chapter are the most commonly encountered and play the largest role in contextualizing empirical studies within existing research traditions.

These theories are also the most likely to undergo change as a consequence of their application in the sociotechnical arena.

Relevant theories exist within multiple interconnected realms. First, there is the realm of political theory, usually focusing on public discourse and what enables it. Second is the realm of social capital and how it is generated and utilized through interaction. Third is the realm of network effects, the definition of the self as part of a set of networks, the identification of the scope of participants that make up networks, and the process of information diffusion through networks. Fourth are theories of motivation and human agency concerning why people do what they do. Fifth is media effect theory, including how agendas are set and frame discourse. Understanding social media and civic engagement requires dipping into each theoretical realm as necessary to support a comprehensive view of these innovative sociotechnical tools supporting such fundamental human activity.

CHAPTER 4

Engagement

One of the great promises of the internet was the possibility that it could serve as a new type of public commons in which political dialog would flourish, citizens would come to understand each other better, and democratic practices such as voting would be more informed. Social media seemed to offer unique affordances for realizing this possibility. But what has actually happened is much more complex. In this chapter, we discuss discourse-supporting applications on the internet, starting with blogs and online forums and focusing most heavily on social media, as they have been used in electoral politics and political activism.

If social media is a new kind of public sphere, then the question arises how it impacts participation in electoral affairs. This question has been addressed in many ways, both in democratic and nondemocratic contexts. In democracies, researchers have been concerned with how social media participation influences voter turnout, enthusiasm and knowledge about candidates and issues, and willingness to participate in offline activism. In less democratic contexts, researchers have been interested in how social media might support dialog and networking.

Foot and Schneider (2002) argued that the emerging use of the web in politics would change the nature of the electoral process. They identified several characteristics of early web use in politics.

- **Coproduction:** The intermingling of content produced by multiple actors. For example, a major media outlet might intermingle their reporting content with emails from citizens. At that time, combining content from multiple applications, for example including a chat feature on a candidate website, was considered to be a form of coproduction. Also, links from one site to another, especially links from a political candidate to an opposition candidate, were considered a novel form of coproduction.

- **Carnival:** Transgressive content such as sarcasm, jesting, insults, and derogatory humor appeared in the earliest political sites on the internet. Examples at the time included websites enabling users to virtually slap a candidate or listen to candidate messages out of context.

- **Mobilization:** Persuasive content meant to encourage others to action was an early feature of internet use by political campaigns, candidates, and advocacy groups. Of course, primary forms of action advocacy were voting, contributing, and demonstrating.

In interviews, Foot and Schneider (2002) found that many types of individuals, "including journalists, campaign professionals, candidates, activists, and citizens," were changing their strategies and behaviors to include this new form of political participation. They foresaw that this technology would result in greater intermingling of content and flattening of communication and expression hierarchies. Ultimately, Foot and Schneider (2002, 2006) famously declared 2000 to be the first "internet election."

During the U.S. election of 2000, a field test referred to as "Web, White and Blue" was conducted of what might be considered an early version of web-based election information tools. In the six months before the election, several news media organizations, internet portals, and content aggregators collaborated to provide links to political organizations and electoral information. During the six weeks leading up to the election, several presidential campaigns (Harry Browne, Patrick Buchanan, George Bush, Al Gore, John Hagelin, and Howard Phillips) agreed to participate in a "Rolling Cyber Debate" by posting a "Message of the Day" and responding to a "Question a Day" posed by citizens. The effort did receive a moderate amount of attention and even showed increasing concentration of interest in the ultimate winner (George Bush) as the election approached. Interview data (Lupia, 2001) suggested that both citizens and campaigns that engaged with Web, White and Blue found it to be an informative and trustworthy new frontier for internet politics, although these results were certainly influenced by positive response bias. There was no evaluation beyond self-report on whether interaction with the project increased engagement or led to voting. However, many participants in a laboratory experiment with the site reported that they had changed their views on a candidate. This was taken as early evidence for the possibility that the internet would play an important role in political participation, as indeed it has.

There have been many studies of the use of the internet in politics prior to the advent of social media (Barber, Mattson and Peterson, 1997; Kluver et al., 2007; Tedesco, 2004; Norris, 2000, 2003), but the introduction of social media was a watershed event (Graham et al., 2013; Hendricks, and Denton Jr., 2010; Stromer-Galley, 2014). Social media connects people with political information in new ways (Hemphill, Otterbacher, and Shapiro, 2013b; Himelboim, McCreery, and Smith, 2013), and the rise of social media has had an impact on virtually all of the processes associated with the democratic political process.

SNSs are used by politicians to communicate with constituents, by voters to discuss candidates and electoral issues, by citizens to communicate with politicians, and by advocacy groups to influence opinions and voting. Research questions surrounding the use of social media in elections include whether they matter, whether they are different from previous practices, how platforms differ, how their use differs cross-culturally, and how practices have changed over time.

4.1   POLITICAL PARTICIPATION

There have been a number of studies attempting to determine whether or not social media influences levels of participation. Technology optimists claim that social media can be used to increase political participation (Hendricks and Denton, 2010; Norris, 2001; Papacharissi, 2002). Technology pessimists, on the other hand, suggest that social media may harm participation (Baumgartner and Morris, 2010; Bimber, 2001; Putnam, 2000). When considering the question of political engagement, it is important to recognize that there can be may levels of involvement ranging from liking a post ("slacktivism") to actively joining a campaign (Bimber and Davis, 2003). Also, different types of digital media have different influences on knowledge and participation. For example, according to Dimitrova et al. (2014), simple exposure to information in digital media (online news and social media) does not lead to more knowledge, but using social media sites of political parties leads to greater political activity such as going to a rally or meeting or talking with someone else about a political issue. Boulianne (2015a) also found that, for younger people, exposure to online news did not increase knowledge or engagement but that it did increase issue awareness. Issue awareness in turn led to greater probability of low-commitment engagement such as voting or boycotting.

Another way in which use of social media may increase civic engagement is that it allows for leveraging social network ties. One ramification of this effect is that the size of a social network is correlated with the probability of being exposed to political information (Gil de Zúñiga, Jung, and Valenzuela, 2012; Tang and Lee, 2013). Another is that the presence of weak ties in a social network leads to exposure to a greater diversity of opinion (Boulianne, 2015a; McPherson, Smith-Lovin, and Brashears, 2006).

Bimber and Copeland (2013) undertook one of the few studies to examine the relationship between use of digital media and political participation across several critical years in the emergence of social media (1998–2008). Noting many inconsistencies in the literature on this topic, they hypothesized that the contexts in which political activity were taking place were more critical than the medium itself in predicting several dependent measures, i.e., persuading others, donating money, attending a political event, and working on a campaign. Most important for the study of social media, they noted a discontinuity in their data that appeared around the introduction and broad uptake of social media. Before 2004, they claim that there is no consistent relationship between digital media use and measures of participation. However, after that the relationships do become more consistent. Especially strong was the effect that use of digital media had on the dependent measure of persuading others. The years 2004 and 2008, corresponding to the emergence of social media, saw dramatic increases in this measure. Since social media does afford deliberation, this finding is tantalizing and consistent with the speculations of others about the relationship between the internet and deliberation (Cho et al., 2009; Xenos and Moy, 2007). In 2008, individuals using digital media showed a greater probability of attending a political event and of working on a campaign, but since this is a singular finding, the authors are more circumspect in interpreting it.

In an extensive study of a range of social media tools (Twitter, Facebook, YouTube, and MySpace) and other electronic participation tools (email, website, iPhone app) used by the 2008

Obama campaign, Cogburn and Espinoza-Vasquez (2011) claim that the successful use of social media by the 2008 campaign was subsequently carried across into the administration via sites such as Transition.gov and Change.gov, and that this constituted the beginnings of a "network nation," or a group of civically engaged citizens who were connected to each other electronically and who continued to be informed about, and to in turn provide opinion and engage in discourse about political issues in the new government.

Social media may influence participation by exposing people to diverse news from their contacts (Dimitrova et al., 2014; Gil de Zúñiga, Copeland, and Bimber, 2013; Holt et al., 2013; Messing and Westwood, 2014; Morris and Morris, 2013; Pasek, Moore, and Romer, 2009), exposing people to news from trusted contacts (Bode, 2012), exposing non-politically oriented people to political news (Bucy and Gregson, 2001), exposing people to political news incidentally when they are doing something else (Douglas et al., 2014; Pasek, Moore, and Romer, 2009; Tang and Lee, 2013; Xenos, Vromen, and Loader, 2014), exposing people to more information because increased network size provides more opportunities to view mobilizing information (Gil de Zúñiga, Jung, and Valenzuela, 2012; Tang and Lee, 2013), or because of participation contagion (Klofstad, 2011; Pancer et al., 2007; Vitak et al., 2011). In a meta-analysis of 36 studies, Boulianne (2015b) found that the majority (82%) of measures of relationship between social media use and civic engagement were positive. This effect was strongest for civic participation involving campaign and election activities and weaker for protest activities. The study was unable to untangle whether this had to do with social network effects or exposure to a greater diversity of news and information (cf. Boulianne, 2009, Dalrymple and Scheufele, 2007; Tolbert and McNeal, 2003). These findings are consistent with earlier studies on media consumption and civic engagement outside of the context of social media (McLeod, Scheufele, and Moy, 1999).

Lack of the interactive and prosumer features of Web 2.0 technologies has been shown to decrease the appeal of civic engagement sites (Coleman 2007, 2008). Coleman (2008) contrasted engagement sites that were built with user autonomy in mind to ones that were more top-down and found that sites which attempt to manage user experiences are less conducive to engagement. He suggests that this reflects a philosophical difference in developers' attitudes, with one emphasizing the need to structure and guide behavior and the other emphasizing exploratory and imaginative modes of engagement.

Bennett (2007, 2008) and his colleagues (Bennett, Wells and Freelon, 2011) argue that old media, including internet models prior to social media, support "dutiful citizenship" whereas new social media supports "actualizing citizenship." Dutiful citizenship is rooted in concepts of responsibility as communicated in a top-down manner from authorities and formal organizations. Actualized citizenship is more open to multiple forms of engagement that are realized though social expression in the context of peer and interest networks. The former has a clear distinction between producers and consumers of information while the latter blurs the distinction, allowing multiple parties to coproduce and co-interpret civic actions, political news, and other public matters:

> *"This citizenship typology enables us to think about a generational shift away from taking cues as members of groups or out of regard for public authorities (opinion leaders, public officials, and journalists), and toward looser personal engagement with peer networks that pool (crowd source) information and organize civic action using social technologies that maximize individual expression"* (Bennett, Wells and Freelon, 2011, p. 839).

A recently described phenomenon of "hashtag drift" in political contexts on Twitter is interesting in light of the concept of "actualizing citizenship." Hashtag drift occurs when individuals begin to use a hashtag in more diverse and individualistic ways than it was originally intended (Booten, 2016). Booten (2016) described how several political hashtags in Tumblr, originally focused on a specific event or individual, came to be used in more contexts over time. He found that this was not just a community-level phenomenon, but also that individual users of the social media tool also exhibited hashtag drift, suggesting that they were expanding their own sense of what a set of hashtags meant and appropriating them for their own expressive purposes. Bennett and Segerberg (2011) suggest that this type of appropriation is a healthy and novel form of collective action enabled by social media.

4.2   CANDIDATES, POLITICIANS, AND POLITICAL PARTIES

The earliest uses of the internet by U.S. politicians can be traced to the 1990s (Davis, 1999; Klinenberg and Perrin, 2000; Stromer-Galley, 2000). In that period, available interactive and transactional aspects of the internet were not used by politicians, and the predominant mode of interaction with the public was to post selected emails and responses on politicians' brochure-like websites (Kamark, 1999). Once social media began to enjoy wide adoption, politicians and candidates for political office were quick to adopt it for their campaign activities (Abroms and Lefebvre, 2009; Church, 2010; Conway, Kenski, and Wang, 2013, 2015). In the U.S., 2008 is considered to be a pivot year in the use of SNSs in political campaigns (Johnson and Perlmutter, 2010). Candidate Barack Obama utilized social media and microblogging to significant effect in the 2008 U.S. presidential election (Hendricks and Denton, 2010). Several researchers, in fact, credit the success of Obama's first presidential campaign to strategic and effective use of multiple social media platforms (Cogburn and Espinoza-Vasquez, 2011; Fraser and Dutta, 2008). Cogburn and Espinoza-Vasquez (2011) note that the Obama campaign "used Facebook to organize, Twitter to send news, and YouTube to communicate" (p. 201).

Although minor political parties were early adopters of the internet, the major U.S. political parties began to make use of it around 2000, leading to what Margolis and Resnick (2000) described as a "normalization of politics" on the internet. Contrary to many digital optimists, Margolis, Resnick, and Wolfe (1999) argued that internet campaigning at that time had no novel qualities, instead serving only to make existing power inequalities more difficult to overcome. What has come to be called the "normalization hypothesis" in digital politics contrasts with the "innovation hypothesis," that new media technologies lead to fundamental changes in the electoral process (Cornfield, 2004; Kaid, 2006; Schweitzer, 2008).

Facebook use by U.S. politicians running for office has increased steadily from Facebook's inception to the present. The period of 2006–2008 is widely considered to be a breakout year for use of social media in U.S. elections. In 2006, in a feature called *Election Pulse*, Facebook produced pages for all U.S. members of Congress and candidates and offered them for use by the politicians (Williams and Gulati, 2013). In a similar move, YouTube entered U.S. politics in 2012 by offering a "Politics" channel, hosting a Town Hall meeting with President Obama, and co-sponsoring the 2012 debates with CNN.

Although candidates had already widely adopted web pages, the advent of social media created a situation in which constituents, pro and con, could comment on the sites of candidates and potentially receive the attention of campaigns to their concerns. According to Williams and Gulati (2013), 32% of the candidates running for the Senate and 13% of candidates running for the House updated their social media profiles. Candidates in highly contested races, candidates with more money, and non-incumbents were the most likely to use their Facebook profiles. Democrats were also initially more interested in social media than Republicans. Evans, Cordova, and Sipole (2014) reported that over 80% of U.S. congressional candidates in 2012 had Twitter accounts.

Despite the optimism reflected in the innovation hypothesis, studies of the strategies of candidates using social media have mostly shown that they are similar to earlier broadcast strategies (although Stromer-Galley (2014) suggests that challengers tend to be more creative users of social media than incumbents—with perhaps the prototypical example being Obama in 2008 (Hendricks and Denton Jr., 2010)). Specifically, candidates, politicians, and parties use social media to attack opponents, push an agenda, and boast about candidates' character and accomplishments (Devlin, 2005; Druckman, Kifer, and Parkin, 2009; Rossini, et al., 2017). Golbeck, Grimes, and Rogers (2010) found that over half (53%) of a sample of tweets from various periods in 2009 produced by members of Congress were essentially press releases, primarily policy statements and facts. Another 27% were about politicians' locations and activities, usually promoting upcoming events. These tweets, which constituted the large majority of posts, were often accompanied by links to actual press releases, news stories, or websites located elsewhere on the internet. Only 4% of the sample data had any personal content, only 3% constituted requests for action, and only 1% was used for fundraising. Similar results were found by the same researchers for tweets by members of Parliament in the United Kingdom.

Hemsley, Tanupabrungsun, and Semaan (2017) examined tweets from U.S. gubernatorial candidates in 2014 and through content analysis arrived at the following categories.

- **Advocacy:** Candidates describe a position on an issue and proves a positive view of themselves.

- **Informative:** Candidates state a fact in a non-persuasive manner.

- **Call to Action:** Candidates ask their audience to do something such as attend a rally, volunteer for an activity, watch a video, or donate money.

- **Attack:** Candidates depict an opponent in a negative light.

- **Conversational:** Candidates respond to a previous tweet.

- **Ceremonial:** Tweets about holidays and official events.

In results similar to Golbeck, Grimes, and Rogers (2010), they found that the majority of tweets were in the advocacy (31%) and informative (29%) categories. Contrary to the prior study, however, they found a large percentage of tweets in the call-to-action category (23%), probably because these tweets were collected in the context of elections.

4.2.1   AUDIENCE AND MICROTARGETING

Social media creates a dilemma for politicians since they prefer targeted messaging, and social media is notorious for loss of audience and message control (Gueorguieva, 2008; Johnson and Perlmutter, 2010; Marwick and boyd, 2011; Stromer-Galley, 2000). Despite the potential for more direct and personal networking between politicians/candidates and citizens, Stromer-Galley (2014) finds that political campaigns prefer to keep tight control over their messaging. Since adopting social media platforms in earnest, politicians now employ significant social media teams to monitor and manipulate multiple social media streams for both office holders and candidates. According to Kreiss (2014), in 2012 the Romney and Obama social media teams actively set agendas and framed discussion on Twitter with multiple audiences in mind including supporters and journalists. Kreiss (2014) found that the greater autonomy given to social media staffers by the Obama campaign allowed them to respond in a more agile manner to breaking political events and influence how others perceived ongoing situations.

The audiences for politicians and campaigns are both potential voters and traditional media (Kenski and Conway, 2016; Parmelee, 2013), although the relationship between social media and traditional media is complicated, with each borrowing from the other (Conway, Kenski, and Wang, 2015; Jungherr, 2014).

Social media enables voter microtargeting, or the identification of very small groups of special-interest voters and tailoring of messaging specifically to them. On the one hand, microtargeting is a way to guarantee that messages reach the most receptive and interested audiences. On the other hand, microtargeted messages hide information from voters who are not targeted, thereby limiting the broader electorate's exposure to diverse viewpoints and precluding them from becoming interested in something they have not been previously identified as caring about (Barocas, 2012). Taken to an extreme, a microtargeted campaign is an asymmetrical information environment in which "[T]he candidate knows everything about the voter, but the media and the public know nothing about what the candidate really believes" (Gertner, 2004). Microtargeted information is likely to be more extreme and divisive than information directed at a broader audience (Hillygus and Shields, 2008). This can result in a more fragmented electorate that is responding to highly individualized and personalized messages instead of broad, societal matters (Pariser, 2011; Steitz and Quinn, 2007).

Microtargeting is sure to become a more thoroughly studied phenomenon now that the U.S. election of 2016 has taken place. In that election, mature microtargeting technology that used extensive social media mining and profiling was deployed more extensively than ever before (at the time this is being written, Facebook is embroiled in a significant scandal involving use of their data by the data analytics firm Cambridge Analytica.)

4.2.2   AGENDA SETTING AND FRAMING

Framing is the process of creating a prior knowledge state that influences the interpretation of subsequent information. Framing has been studied extensively in political discourse (Scheufele and Tewksbury, 2007), especially with regard to the role of media in shaping opinions and attitudes. Social media can often serve as a framing mechanism for news and information. Agenda setting is the process of creating a topic of widespread attention and interest within the media. Social media has introduced a new dynamic for agenda setting and framing such that individuals outside of the traditional media can focus a large audience on a topic or influence their interpretation (Boyntin and Richardson, 2015; Shapiro and Hemphill, 2014).

Hemphill, Culotta, and Heston (2013a) studied the use of Twitter hashtags by politicians to frame their tweets. They showed that politicians strategically use hashtags to highlight certain aspects of issues, and they argue that this encourages "frame alignment," or increased consistency of beliefs with others with whom we are acquainted (Kim and Bearman, 1997). Frame alignment may happen in social media because social media users follow others like them (Himelboim, McCreery, and Smith, 2013) and are thus subject to frequent and persistent framing of issues along the same ideological positions.

Shapiro and Hemphill (2014) examined whether policy topics being highlighted in traditional media (the *New York Times*) were simultaneously being highlighted on Twitter. They found that policy issues did co-occur on Twitter and in the *NYT*, however they were unable to obtain evidence about the direction of causality and therefore could not address a claim by Parmelee (2013) that politicians use tweets to set agendas which are then picked up by traditional media.

In the end, social media may not be a good medium for attracting new supporters (Baumgartner and Morris, 2010; Zhang et al., 2009). Only a small proportion of social media users actually use these platforms to follow politicians (Smith, 2011), and research suggests that candidates do not attract many new followers by using social media (Conway, Kenski and Wang, 2013). Still, social media may be good for inspiring existing supporters.

4.3   CITIZENS, CONSTITUENTS, AND VOTERS

Politicians are not the only ones to utilize the internet, and social media, for political purposes. In fact, the new possibilities offered to citizens by these technologies are potentially the most revolutionary. The internet allows citizens to find information from a broader range of sources, and on a broader range of topics, than ever before. Social technologies have also allowed individuals to express themselves to a broader audience and have resulted in the development of political information sharing networks with distinct and interesting features. In addition to enhanced information-seeking abilities, social technologies have allowed citizens to (apparently) address politicians more directly, and to engage in political discourse with each other.

4.3.1   INFORMATION SEEKING

A uses and gratifications study of internet use to learn about politics (Kaye and Johnson, 2002) identified four motivations for seeking out political information online.

- **Guidance** involves seeking information in order to make a specific decision, such as who to vote for. Guidance also involves learning about the characteristics of political candidates and about issues. People seeking guidance are often looking for balanced or unbiased points of view.

- **Information seeking/surveillance** is a purposeful form of internet browsing that involves keeping up with the issues of the day and following trends as they develop.

- **Entertainment** is an emotional motivation that involves obtaining relaxation, excitement, amusement, relief and other forms of emotional consequence.

- **Social utility** involves gathering information that will be helpful in discussions of political issues with others or in participating in political discourse in general.

High levels of self-efficacy with regard to politics were positively associated with information seeking/surveillance and with entertainment. In other words, individuals who felt more like they could effect change in government were more likely to keep up with political information and find consumption of media related to politics enjoyable. The guidance motivation was negatively correlated with the guidance factor, suggesting that individuals with low trust are more likely to seek political information from the internet.

Search queries have been shown to track reliably to issue salience as measured by news coverage (Granka, 2009, 2013; Weeks and Southwell, 2010) and other measures of public interest (Scheitle, 2011). Weber, Garimella, and Borra (2012) examined queries submitted to the Bing search engine during six months at the end of 2011. They were interested in queries from individuals (anonymized) who issued many searches, suggesting that these people were politically engaged. They further isolated queries in which the searchers clicked on a results link to a political blog, resulting in a corpus of over 8,600 politically relevant queries. They determined the political leaning (left, center, and right) of the queries, based on the political orientation of blogs and Wikipedia entries contained in the larger result sets. They further assigned sentiment values to the queries based on the sentiment (positive and negative) of the content of results sets from the query (cf. Shen et al., 2006).

Their findings showed that queries about Democrats tended to be more right-leaning while queries about Republicans tended to be more left-leaning, showing that there was considerable interest in learning about "the other side." Left-leaning queries also tended to be more positive and less negative. The authors were also able to track changes in the political leaning of queries about particular politicians over time and create timeline visualizations of these changes along with changes in associated topics.

Powell, Richmond, and Williams (2011) compared college students who were members of the social media sites of the two major U.S. presidential candidates in 2008 to college students who were not. They examined credibility, interpersonal attraction, and homophily—three constructs important to voter perceptions of candidates (Wensch, McCroskey, and Richmond, 2008). They found that information seeking was positively associated with interpersonal attraction for members of the Obama social media network, but contrary to expectations (Kitchens, Powell, and Williams, 2003), they also found that information seeking was negatively associated with homophily. In other words, dissimilarity with the candidate led to greater information seeking. They also found that credibility ratings for Obama were higher for people who were members of Obama's social media site then for nonmembers.

Douglas et al. (2014) interviewed Millennials about their use of the Internet and social media to learn about political candidates and further observed their behavior in searches related to a mock election. The Millennials in their study did not seek out political information, but instead ran across it serendipitously while doing other things. When political information was encountered in social media, the participants used the judgments of others, via liking volume, to decide whether to browse the information themselves. Although they sometimes did browse political information, these participants reported being overwhelmed with information generally, and often being annoyed by political information specifically, such they even structure their social networks to avoid political content. When asked specifically to evaluate candidates for political office using information available through Facebook posts and online news, the Millennials used several criteria gleaned both from text and images.

- **Evidence of action:** Participants judged candidates favorably when they saw evidence of community involvement. This was judged by seeing images of politicians working with community groups or reading about their activities. Participants who did not use social media were less concerned with evidence of community involvement.

- **Emotional engagement:** Smiling, shaking hands, and other evidence of emotional engagement with community activities were judged positively by participants looking at social media.

- **Candidate presence:** Although action in the community was seen in the most positive light, simply being there was also counted favorably by social media users.

- **Responsiveness to citizens:** Participants noticed when a candidate responded to social media questions directed toward them or addressed directly issues raised on Facebook. This was taken as evidence of caring and reciprocity and counted favorably.

- **Community assessment:** Participants judged candidates by the types of people who participated in rallies (as evidenced by images) and the types of people who voiced support. Participants noticed grammatical and spelling errors in posts or on supporters' campaign signs and took this as a negative reflection on the candidate.

- **Community support:** Candidates were judged by the amount of support that others displayed for them. Participants discriminated between blind support, or simple cheerleading, and what they considered to be more genuine expressions of support about specific issues.

Douglas et al. (2014) noticed in the context of social media what others had noticed in the context of campaign websites (Dostie-Goulet, 2009; Sundar, Kalyanaraman, and Brown, 2003), namely that the opinions of others are highly important to younger people judging political candidates. The added value of this research, however, was to show the importance of community and reciprocity as evidenced in two-way social media contexts.

4.3.2   CITIZEN-TO-POLITICIAN

A signature feature of social media is that it allows for apparent two-way communication between politicians and citizens. Individuals who do use social media for interacting with politicians and political candidates feel that they are in two-way communication (Bucy and Gregson, 2001) and state that they feel more personally connected to the candidate or politician (Lee and Oh, 2012). Robertson and his colleagues (Robertson et al., 2012, 2013) found that, in the months prior to an election, most Facebook posts on candidates' newsfeeds were directed at the candidates rather than at others. As an election approached, the number of comments directed at candidates diminished as the number of comments directed at other people increased, such that they were about even by the time an election arrived. The researchers identified six primary categories of comments directed at candidates.

- **Question:** Asking the candidate for his or her position on an issue.

- **Suggestion:** Telling the candidate that they should do or try something.

- **Request:** Asking the candidate to do something.

- **Support:** Expressions of enthusiasm and encouragement.

- **Invitation:** Asking the candidate to participate in something.

- **Stories:** Telling personal narratives or describing things that have happened to the poster.

Mascaro, Agosto, and Goggins (2016) examined 28 million unique tweets related to the 2012 U.S. presidential election (53 million tweets counting retweets). They were particularly interested in conversational pairs as indicated by at-reply tags. They noted that the most frequent tweets relevant to the presidential candidates were generated by automated bots, an issue we will return to in Chapter 5. The researchers found that citizens tweeting about the candidates used the at-reply feature to direct their messages to candidates, media, and campaigns, but that these tweets were never reciprocated. Thus, while citizens might have felt that they were communicating with campaigns, there was no evidence that the campaigns were listening. They argue that the public using Twitter in this way is a "phantom public" in the sense that Lippman (1925) described so-called public opinion. They suggest that for social media to be more useful, better filtering mechanisms need to be developed and distractions need to be contained.

Hemphill and Roback (2014) examined tweets from the period of 2011–2013 and extracted tweets directed at candidates about the political issues of SOPA and PIPA (as indicated by hashtags), two online anti-piracy bills. Building on earlier work (Roback and Hemphill, 2013), they categorized comments by constituents to politicians and organized them into several lobbying strategies, the most frequent ones being:

- **Direct opposition/support (17%):** a citizen expresses an opinion about an issue;

- **Promotional (14%):** links to promotional media;

- **FYI (12%):** links to something the citizen thinks a politician should see or know about; and

- **Thank you for opposing/supporting (11%):** expression of gratitude for a politician's position or action.

There were several less frequent comment types, which prompted candidates about their policy positions or encouraged them to take positions in various ways, including:

- **Loaded policy question (6%):** question with a presupposition about the candidate's position;

- **Please oppose/support (4%):** a direct request to take a particular position on an issue;

- **Disappointed (3%):** an negative emotional statement about a candidate's position;

- **General directive (3%):** a request to take some position or another on an issue;

- **What is your position? (3%):** a direct request for a position statement; and

- **I'm your constituent and I oppose (1%):** a statement that a constituent cannot support a candidate because of their stand on an issue.

Hemphill and Robach (2014) use their research to reinforce the point that citizens are not just using social media to "soapbox" about issues, as claimed by Parmelee and Bichard (2013). Rather, constituents addressing their congressional representatives do so in robust and complicated ways in a sincere attempt to influence policy.

4.3.3 CITIZEN-TO-CITIZEN

Political discussion on the internet and within social media can lead to exposure to diverse opinions or contribute to an information bubble reinforced by like-minded acquaintances and selective attention. Stromer-Galley (2003) conducted in-depth interviews with individuals who regularly use online political discussion spaces. Her work suggested strongly that these individuals sought out and enjoyed the diversity of information available to them on the internet. They reported enjoying encountering new political viewpoints, however they also reported disliking negative discourse. Semaan et al. (2015) similarly found individuals using multiple social media platforms to enhance both their own and other people's exposure to diverse information. In fact, several people in that study considered themselves to be "information tailors," engaging in reflection about their audience(s) and strategizing about how to present information effectively. These individuals are similar to the Twitter "opinion leaders" studied by Park (2013), who exhibit high motivations for information seeking, mobilization, and public expression.

Persuasion is a type of civic engagement that is perhaps more widespread in the era of social media (Gil de Zúñiga, Puig-i-Abril, and Rojas, 2009; Xenos, Vromen, and Loader, 2014). Individuals are relying more on their social media connections to learn about political issues (Bode, 2015; Bond et al., 2012; Messing and Westwood, 2014; Turcotte et al., 2015). Social media users find news that had been shared, and hence filtered through others, to be more trustworthy than news that is delivered directly from a media source (Turcotte et al., 2015). Weeks, Arde`vol-Abreu, and Gil de Zúñiga (2015) found that individuals who produce a high frequency of online content in social media, so-called "prosumers," regard themselves as important sources of persuasive information and are often perceived by others as being authoritative.

An, Querica, and Crowcroft (2014) studied partisan sharing of news on Facebook and Twitter. They were interested in whether the selective exposure hypothesis in the context of political news (Goldman and Mutz, 2011; Iyengar and Hahn, 2009), that people prefer news that agrees with their preconceptions and are more likely to share it with others, could be observed in social media news sharing. They found that indeed both liberal and conservative users of these social media sites consume and share news with the same political leaning as their ideological preference, and that they avoid counter-attitudinal news. However, in their data they did find that out of all the political news articles which conservatives shared about 25% were counter-attitudinal. The corresponding value for liberals was 17%. Other analyses tended to suggest that conservatives were less polarized as measured by counter-attitudinal news sharing than liberals, a result consistent with LaCour (2012). They also found that high-volume sharers tended to be more partisan. Interestingly, news sharing related to elections became less partisan as the election approached.

Tumasjan et al. (2010) studied tweets that mentioned a political party or politician in the 2009 German general election. They found a robust debate taking place within Twitter, but noted that it was led by a small number of politically involved individuals who posted with high frequency. The relative number of Tweets for a politician was predictive of the election outcome, with a higher number of Tweets being associated with a higher probability of being elected. This mirrors the findings of Williams and Gulati (2013) that Facebook likes predicted electoral outcomes in the 2008 U.S. presidential primary elections. This is in contrast to studies of internet message boards where a small number of individuals can dominate the discussion, thereby making them non-predictive of campaign popularity or election outcomes (Jansen and Koop, 2005).

Zhou et al. (2010) looked at tweets generated during protests following the 2009 Iranian presidential election. They found that retweet cascades tended to be wide but not deep, meaning that retweets of a particular piece of information were more likely to emanate from a central user to a large number of their immediate followers (up to a thousand) but spread outward through the friend/follower network for only a few nodes (never more than seven). With the great breadth of friend/follower networks in Twitter, a few individuals can have tremendous influence on the spread of information. The most frequent information being spread was breaking news, jokes and sarcasm, self-reflection about the role of Twitter, personal accounts (including images and video), activism, technical help information, and rumors and misinformation.

4.3.4   SOCIAL WATCHING

While many studies focus on a particular social media platform, some researchers have begun to explore the use of multiple platforms simultaneously. Referred to as "second screening," or "social watching," it is now common for many people to combine social media participation with live viewing of an event.

An example would be using Twitter or Facebook to discuss a political debate as it is happening on television. Gorkovenko and Taylor (2016) observed and interviewed British citizens between 18–29 years of age who used Twitter and Facebook while watching televised political debates during the 2015 UK general election. They were interested in the motivations of participants for using social media while watching the debates. A primary motivation was to learn what others thought, which was used as a gauge of "public opinion." Participants paid special attention to what others said was important, using the crowd as a kind of attention director. Twitter was considered superior to Facebook for this purpose because it was perceived as being more real-time. Participants used the comments of others to reflect on their own ideas and opinions, especially seeking out confirming points of view. They did not necessarily ignore contrary perspectives, but often dismissed them as irrelevant or wrong, using the social media stream to reaffirm their own beliefs.

In addition to these *learning* goals, participants also found that the information available from social media *enriched* their experience by making the debates more entertaining and more engaging. They augmented debate content by looking things up and fact checking, creating more of a sense of empowerment through activity as opposed to passive reception of information. There were times when the "second screen" became the primary object of interest and the debate took on a background role, as when people began a conversation among themselves.

Participants found that social media content provided "talking points" that sparked both online and face-to-face discussion. Some participants found that sharing their own opinions provided an ego boost and otherwise positively influenced their perceived social status. However, several participants chose not to post, citing several reasons for passive participation. These reasons had mainly to do with their imagined audience and the fear of provoking someone (cf. Semaan et al., 2014) or violating online etiquette rues such as posting too frequently. Retweeting or reposting the opinions of others created less anxiety. Finally, the participants explained that humor, immediacy, and integrity were the most important factors that influenced the usefulness of social media content.

Maruyama et al. (2017) found that people who actively used Twitter during a debate were more likely to change their vote in response to a candidate's poor performance, and to Twitter comments about the debate winner, than people who were not using Twitter during the same debate. This vote switch was "sticky," persisting for at least two weeks.

In a further study of social watching, Maruyama et al. (2017) conducted an experiment in which the valence of feedback that participants received about comments made on Twitter while watching a political debate was varied. The researchers found that receiving positive feedback on tweets (a "favorite") increased participants' sense of community, and that not receiving feedback on a post led to disappointment. Participants who received favorable feedback on their tweets reported spending more time reflecting on their own opinions and thinking about what to say ("anticipatory discussion elaboration"). Even so, participants who did not actively tweet but instead monitored Twitter activity reported the highest levels of reflection about what they might say. This suggests that "lurking" on social media should be more widely studied as a potential positive activity for learning about political issues and candidates. While there may be some positive influences of social watching, the researchers also found opinion conformity, consistent with other studies on second screening in different contexts (Cameron and Geidner, 2014).

Houston et al. (2013) also studied second screening during two 2012 debates (one presidential debate and one vice-presidential debate). They also found that "live tweeting" had an influence on the perception of the debate, specifically that it resulted in participants paying more careful attention and considering the debates to be more important. The researchers propose that both of these influences may lead to greater civic engagement and to more informed design making (cf. Benoit, Hansen, and Verser, 2003; McKinney and Chattopadhyay, 2007).

4.4   ACTIVISM AND PROTEST

Social media has played a significant role in the practices of activists. An important reason for this is the ability of social media to connect activists outside of official channels of communication and in situations where normal communications are restricted or denied. In terms of civic engagement in the arena of protest and activism, Uldam and Vestergaard (2015) distinguish between formal and informal modes of engagement. Formal modes include widely recognized and usually legal disruptive actions like strikes and boycotts. Informal modes are more spontaneous, often decentralized actions such as disruptive meetups and website hacking.

Social media can serve as an environment through which political will is expressed and collective purpose is nurtured. Crivellaro et al. (2014) examined the posts on a Facebook page devoted to the redevelopment of a derelict pool in the seaside town of Tynemouth, UK. A page that drew little interest initially, the "Friends of Tynemouth Outdoor Pool" Facebook site grew dramatically when the town submitted development plans for public comment. This growth paralleled a growth in the real world in political action, including flash mobs, media campaigns, and other meetings. A discourse analysis of the postings, both textual and image-based, revealed three primary themes relevant to building solidarity around a cause.

- **Memories and nostalgia for the future:** Many posters depicted via text or image stories about the role of the pool in the past history of the town. These were typically accompanied by reminiscences that tied events together into a network of personal local histories. The stories allowed current occupants of the town to imagine themselves and their families as part of a generational tradition. The posts in this category also included counterarguments about the folly of nostalgic desire to return to the past, which in turn created reflective discourse about connections between past and future.

- **Nurturing a political potential:** Discourse in this category involved the expression of the rights of people to criticize the town's management and to envision alternative futures. By asserting their rights to oppose the redevelopment, a solidarity of purpose developed via these discourse threads.

- **Activating the political:** The political power of the collective voices on the Facebook page became recognized as potentially powerful. The authors note that the "mundane" act of liking a page can turn into a politically efficacious act in the aggregate, ultimately underpinning a committed, collective political movement in the real world.

The authors view this type of social media environment as enabling a "cultural voice" (Fraser, 1990). They find that social media spaces can indeed serve as a socio-cultural political context (Dourish, 2010) in which everyday discourse, enabled by the affordances of the social platform, can become an effective resistance movement to counter official power.

The Iranian election protests of 2009 and the "Arab Spring" uprisings in 2011 were the first large political protests during which the use of social media and microblogs, especially Twitter and Facebook, were examined closely by researchers (Burns and Eltham, 2009). Twitter in particular seems to have played an important role in such movements because of the ability of people who were in the midst of situations to be able to live-tweet their observations and experiences. This produced a global audience that would not have otherwise seen these events due to the absence of traditional media. It also produced first-person eyewitness accounts of events that are highly compelling.

Starbird and Palen (2012), studying tweets from the 2011 uprising in Egypt, note that Twitter use during a mass protest works to disperse information from a crowd to a larger audience which then turns around and shows solidarity by extensive retweeting and solidarity responses. Thus, Twitter in such cases works both directions, to inform the audience and to encourage the demonstrators. They also note that the "work" of information diffusion was done by the larger audience. Once information from participants was released on Twitter, its spread was accomplished by members of an audience or retweeters. Thus, spread of information not only disseminates news broadly, but it also serves as an indicator of how important the events are to the larger crowd. Starbird and Palen (2012) also note that there is an important distinction between original information that comes from individuals who are "on the ground," and "derivative" information that is added by the crowd during the process of retweeting (cf. Starbird et al., 2010).

Al-Ani et al. (2012) examined the use of social media during the Egyptian uprisings as an instance of Castells's (2007, 2009) notion of "counter-power," or power in opposition to institutionalized, establishment power structures. In the five-year period leading up to the uprisings the percentage of posts containing personal topics decreased while the percentage containing political topics increased to the point where there were more political tweets (50%) than personal tweets (35%) by 2011. Even the personal tweets changed their nature to focus more on social injustice, for example to give eyewitness accounts of police brutality. The Egyptian government eventually imposed a "virtual curfew" on social media use, enforced through arrest of prominent bloggers and control of ISPs, however the number of information providers and retweeters was too large to control and many were able to work around ISP restrictions by using cell phones and friends' accounts outside of Egypt. These researchers suggest that in contrast to the expected use of social media to make calls for action, the primary function was to create a "counter narrative" about what was actually happening. They refer to this as an alternative public space that facilitates horizontal, many-to-many communication channels as opposed to a vertical channel flowing from official media.

Karkın et al. (2015) used critical discourse analysis (van Dijk, 2001, 2006) to examine the tweets of politicians during the 2013 Taksim Gezi Park protests in Turkey. A plan to redesign the park, located in Istanbul, triggered a local sit-in. The violent ejection of demonstrators participating in the sit-in resulted in a larger movement that ultimately spread across Turkey. Themes of the larger movement included protest against increasing restrictions on freedom of assembly, increasing media censorship, use of excessive force and violation of civil rights, and other anti-authoritarian sentiments. Social media played a significant role in the formation and maintenance of this movement. It was used both by protestors and by politicians, the latter being both the government in power and the opposition. Karkın et al. (2015) found that politicians utilized all of the political discourse strategies identified by van Dijk (2006). Both government and opposition politicians used mostly "actor categorizations and descriptions," which are statements that describe themselves, usually in a positive manner (e.g., "We are on the side of truth") or others, usually in a negative manner (e.g., "They are killers"). These statements are identified by the use of pronouns such as "we," "us," "they," and "them." Opposition politicians were more likely to generate tweets in the category of "burden/victimization," which are statements about negative consequences of actions (e.g., "Their suppression only results in angering more people"). Opposition politicians were also more likely to generate tweets in the category of "lexicalization/metaphor," which use symbolic language or references to thematic types ("like a bride and groom") or historical individuals or events.

Another common discourse strategy used by both sides was "distancing/disclaimers," or the brief mention of a good feature of the other side followed by exclusive focus on negative attributes (e.g., "some are truthful, but most are deceitful"), and generalizations, often about the other side ("Most of them have no moral compass"). Their primary point is that politicians used Twitter in this case to polarize the audience by demonizing the other and praising the in-group using well-known political discourse strategies, in this case expressed in 140-character tweets.

Wang and Mark (2013) note that in authoritarian situations where news is censored, people rely more on each other as news sources and for information about how much to trust information. Thus, news that spreads via social media is important (cf. Al-ani et al., 2012). Kavanaugh et al. (2016) surveyed young Tunisians about their use of social media for news and information during the 2011 Tunisian uprising. They found that reliability ratings for information obtained from photo and video sharing sites, Facebook, and internet news were as high as face-to-face reliability ratings, which were all much higher than reliability ratings for newspapers, radio, and television. In general, television, radio, newspapers, and government information were grouped together as the least independent, and thus the least reliable, sources of information. Video sharing, Facebook, internet news, and face-to-face information sharing grouped together as the most reliable sources of information. Twitter and television talk shows formed a third category of information source also not considered highly reliable, possibly because these sources were non-informative in terms of information and were highly loaded with reaction and emotion information. The most shared information came from Facebook, YouTube, and Twitter.

Wulf et al. (2013a) observed and interviewed political activists in a Palestinian village who were using a variety of methods, including social media, to organize demonstrations against Israel's settlement policy. Their in-depth ethnographic study spanned a two-year period (2010–2012) that began before the village had internet access. Activists were aware of the power of social media in spreading word of their cause, and they played an important role in bringing the internet into the village. Within this time period, the village went from essentially archiving photos on a single person's cell phone which they shared in face-to-face encounters to creating and maintaining several personal Facebook pages and a group page devoted to news and information about the resistance. The latter, created and maintained by a 13-year-old boy, was supported by a primitive internet infrastructure that reached only a few locations in the village. Personal Facebook pages combined political activism with more personal matters. The goals of Arabic versus English posts were apparently different, with Arabic posts being more factual and descriptive, and containing calls for action, whereas English posts were more ideological and directed at calls for compassion and understanding. Despite significant technical handicaps, a handful of local activists in this situation ultimately developed a sophisticated and organized social media strategy that was coordinated with resistance actions and was used both for local organization and for dissemination of information to the outside world.

Kow et al. (2016) studied a more technologically complex situation in the Umbrella Movement that took place in Hong Kong in 2014. The Umbrella Movement was a set of sit-ins and boycotts, organized primarily by students but ultimately joined by many others, to protest the nomination process for Hong Kong's chief executive. The protestors utilized multiple media platforms including Facebook, WhatsApp, Firechat, Telegram, and Google Docs to disseminate information and coordinate their activities.

Interviews with participants revealed that different media platforms served different purposes. Facebook carried the public discourse and was used to express solidarity through actions such as coordinated profile picture changes. The mobile-phone centered instant messaging app WhatsApp was used to mobilize existing social networks into action via private conversations. WhatsApp also served as a communication conduit through which individuals in the midst of a protest action communicated with coordinators who were outside of the action. Action schedules and classes on how to conduct civic protests were set up in Google Docs and then shared through Facebook. Experimental use of FireChat, which uses Bluetooth technology, thereby avoiding the internet entirely, and Telegram, which has non-persistent chat features, took place to circumvent attempts by authorities to shut down internet and mobile services, or attempts to surveil communications.

In this technology-rich environment, protestors set up and managed a socio-technical protest ecology to serve their multiple purposes, both to directly conduct and coordinate protest actions and also to create what Kow et al. (2016) call "undercurrents," or "persistent activities that exist before and after a social movement, encompassing people's personal networks, ecologies of resources, and free spaces" (p. 3890).

Kow, et al. (2016) suggest that there are four primary uses of social media for social movements:

- information seeking and dissemination;

- frame articulation;

- expression of solidarity; and

- development of counter-narratives.

Information seeking is often observed during disaster or crisis situations (Olteanu, Vieweg, and Castillo, 2015; Qu et al., 2011; Sarcevic et al., 2012; Shklovski, Palen, and Sutton, 2008; Starbird and Palen, 2011), and is a self-explanatory use of social media for the purposes of learning about gaining a larger perspective.

Frame articulation (Snow, 2004) involves pulling together sometimes disparate actions, organizations, and events into a meaningful conceptual whole that supports a movement or ideology. This can be as straightforward as coming up with a collective label for a movement, or it can evolve from prolonged interaction with and participation in social media discourses (Dimond et al., 2013). Expression of solidarity is increasingly common in social media, and often involves a symbolic action that like-minded supporters of a cause take. The prototypical example is the coordinated modification of profile pictures in Facebook (State and Adamic, 2015).

Finally, development of counter-narratives involves the expression of alternative perspectives, often in conflict with official reports (Al-Ani et al., 2012; Monroy-Hernández et al., 2013). The latter is becoming more important and prevalent as the issue of "fake news" takes center stage in the realm of social media and politics.

A participatory, ethnographic study of Global Justice activists involved in a "Stop G8" protest in June 2013 found intriguing cracks in the use of new media technologies in activism (Waddell, Millard, and Saunders, 2014). While social and mobile technologies were used widely by protestors, many activists reported an increasing personalization of information dissemination to protestors' friends and followers in contrast to a broader social movement. The researchers also found that activists were increasingly relying on information collected and disseminated by the public during protest events, not on information collected by their own activists. They refer to this as "public appropriation" of protest events. Finally, a considerable amount of attention was being paid by activists to the use of accessible social and mobile information by nation states and companies for their own ends, resulting in discussion of what *not* to say in such forums. Echoing Habermas's concern with the commercialization of the public sphere, the study concluded that "some activists now see the Web as a socio-technical construct symbolic not of change, but of the deepening entrenchment within the social, economic and political systems they seek to change" (p. 270).

4.5   SUMMARY

The internet, and social media platforms in particular, have changed participation both with regard to civic discourse and democratic elections and also with regard to protests and activism. The connection between social media and engagement is complicated, but most studies suggest that social media increases exposure to diverse viewpoints and can encourage participation. In social media, citizens feel free to address politicians directly and, correctly or not, feel that their voices are heard and that they have a closer relationship with politicians. Politicians, on the other hand, have been slow to use non-broadcast and untraditional modes of interaction afforded by social media.

Outside of the election arena, social media is extremely important to the organization of protest movements and coordination of their activities. It is used not only to coordinate activities, but also to strengthen ideological bonds. The use of social media tools in protest and activism is highly innovative, with users combining multiple information and communication technologies in real time. Surveillance of users of these technologies during protests, and interference in their activities by governments, police, and military is a highly active area of technical and political innovation at the moment. Few studies yet exist on impacts of and reactions to these countermeasures.

CHAPTER 5

Challenges

In this chapter, we explore the downside of social technologies with respect to the health of the polity and its citizens. These concerns can be organized into several themes: homophily and polarization; equity; transparency and trust; and fake news, misinformation and propaganda.

5.1 HOMOPHILY AND POLARIZATION

Many scholars view discussion on the Internet, and social media in particular, as having the qualities of an "echo chamber" in which similar views are sought and shared (Agre, 2002; Colleoni, Rozza, and Arvidsson, 2014; Gilbert, Bergstrom, and Karhalios, 2009; Sunstein, 2007; Wallsten, 2011). Selective exposure has been shown to lead to greater opinion polarization (Sunstein, 2002), suggesting that if it is found on the internet, then the idea that the internet is a productive public sphere is in doubt. Adamic and Glance (2005) published one of the earliest demonstrations of this phenomenon in the space of political blogs, showing that conservative and liberal bloggers tended to link within their respective ideological spheres, although they did find a determined set of cross-linking bloggers. Subsequently, researchers have found that comments following a blog post tend to be supportive and in agreement with the ideology of the post (Gilbert, Bergstrom, and Karahalios, 2009).

The issue whether the internet, and social ICTs in particular, create a situation in which people network primarily with others like themselves is referred to as *homophily* (McPherson, Smith-Lovin, and Cook, 2001). Homophily can be based on many surface features such as similarity in age, ethnic background, and sociographic status, but most important for civic engagement is homophily based on common beliefs or moral values (Kossinets and Watts, 2009). In general, a society in which individuals are not exposed to the opinions of others is not healthy, and many have been concerned that ICTs exacerbate the problem (Putnam, 2000). In the context of e-government and civic engagement, homophily, if it exists to a significant degree, means less exposure to alternative points of view and the absence of opinion diversity.

"Diversity seeking" is considered to be a core value important to good citizenship (Delli Carpini, Cook, and Jacobs, 2004). However, many citizens do not seem to share this view, a problem which Kim and Pasek (2016) call the "diversity deficit." They point out that although the internet allows people access to multiple points of view, and systems are available to encourage diverse information seeking in political information realms (Munson, Lee, and Resnick, 2013; Park et al., 2009), if people do not have a core value that drives them to seek diverse information all of these efforts are for naught.

Unfortunately, many people actively resist being exposed to perspectives that are counter to their own beliefs and actively use search tools and other online tools to avoid it (Garrett, 2009; Knobloch-Westerwick and Meng 2009; Kobayashi et al., 2009). Grevet, Terveen, and Gilbert (2014) found that Facebook users with many friends, who might otherwise be exposed to multiple viewpoints, sometimes avoided the platform during events where high levels of disagreement were possible—political debates for example. They also found that Facebook users actively avoided posting on political topics because they would be controversial, and that when Facebook users did engage in confrontational political discourse they had very little change of changing anyone's mind.

According to several studies, Twitter users tend to re-tweet posts from others with the same political orientation (Boutet, Kim, and Yoneki, 2012; Conover et al., 2011). Conover et al. (2011) showed that retweets show partisan homogeneity with content being divided into left and right political ideologies, however mentions do not form such a polarized network. It is interesting that these two diffusion mechanisms on the same platform result in different network topologies. On the other hand, there is some evidence in this work that cross-ideological mentions are often responses to unwanted or unappreciated tweets, and that mentions are more directed at countering the contrasting point of view as opposed to disseminating it broadly to others.

The internet may restrict exposure to diverse points of view because of selective friendships (Bimber and Davis, 2003; Davis, 1999; Galston, 2003; Mutz and Martin, 2001; Noveck, 2000) and self-selection of information with which people already agree (Adamic and Glance, 2005; Mutz and Martin, 2001), leading to polarization (Stroud, 2010). In fact, some researchers suggest that selective exposure leads to even greater polarization when people take comfort in the fact that others share their viewpoint (Sunstein, 2008). Kelly, Fisher, and Smith (2005) go so far as to call the internet an "anti-commons," suggesting that the metaphor of a public commons is highly misleading in understanding online deliberation. Many of these researchers find that cross-ideological discourse online is often highly argumentative and emotionally charged, especially in the realm of politics.

In contrast to the echo chamber phenomenon, other researchers have found evidence that many people seek out diverse information online. People differ in their interest in the accuracy of information, and sometimes seek out diverse information in an attempt to learn the truth (Hart et al., 2009). A large-sample interview by Horrigan, Garrett, and Resnick (2004) found that people were not just seeking confirming information when they perused news online and that they often encountered opinions counter to their own (cf. Coleman, Morrison, and Anthony, 2011). Stromer-Galley (2003) found in self reports that individuals say they are diversity seeking. Munson and Resnick (2010) described different types of individuals, some being "diversity seeking" while others are "challenge averse." The latter cannot easily be enticed (via systems designed to find, highlight, or otherwise present challenging information) to view information inconsistent with their prior beliefs.

Semann et al. (2014) interviewed individuals who were politically involved online and who read and posted on multiple social media platforms. These selected individuals actively sought alternative viewpoints and thought of it as their responsibility to disseminate multiple perspectives on their own social media channels. They valued diverse opinion but did not like disrespectful posts. Interestingly, these individuals found it difficult to integrate their interest in diverse political discourse with other types of discourse often found on social media, especially in the context of family and like-minded friends. They were very aware of how others might perceive them, and were concerned that their interest in other points of view would be viewed negatively by friends and family. Some even used different tools for political discussion versus social interaction with friends.

Exposure to diverse information increases on the internet at least partly because of inadvertent exposure (Brundidge, 2010; Holt, 2004; Wojcieszak and Mutz, 2009), and people who maintain more diverse networks are exposed to a greater diversity of opinions and perspectives (Scheufele et al., 2006; Yardi and boyd, 2010). In a study of Twitter conversations about a controversial topic (the shooting of an abortion provider), Yardi and boyd (2010) examined exchanges between like-minded individuals and contrasted them with exchanges between individuals who differed in their perspective on the issue. They found both homophily and its opposite, heterogeneity, but noted that these differing exchanges had different purposes and outcomes. Like-minded individuals emerged with greater group identity, whereas ingroup/outgroup affiliations were reinforced after exchanges between people with different opinions.

Research suggests that HCI design can influence the degree to which people seek diverse opinions (Munson and Resnick, 2010). Liao and Fu (2014), for example, found that including indicators of valence and magnitude of an argument or opinion along with the usual title and summary information in search result lists led to greater interest in attitude-challenging information, but only for people who had higher "accuracy motives," or a desire to fully understand an issue. They also found that attitude-challenging information had greater impact if it was presented in a moderate, as opposed to an extreme, manner.

Kriplean et al. (2012) designed a system called "ConsiderIt," which presents users with pro and con arguments relevant to ballot measures. A widespread deployment during a real election resulted in users authoring more arguments from both supporting and opposing perspectives and in users addressing opposing points of view in their own comments. However, users of ConsiderIt did not rate the opposing points to which they were exposed as being more helpful.

Ultimately, there is no single generalization that can be made about the echo chamber effect and polarization. The nature of the medium, the affordances or the tools, the style of argument, and the inclinations of the people involved all interact.

In a massive study of 10 million Facebook users who were willing to share their political affiliation, Bakshy, Messing, and Adamic (2015) found that 18%–20% of users' networks consisted of people with opposing political ideologies. Twenty-four percent (for liberals) and 35% (for conservatives) of shared news on friend networks was found to be cross-cutting with regard to political orientation, however after algorithmic ranking that partially determines ordering in newsfeeds the likelihood of encountering cross-cutting information fell to 8% for liberals and 5% for conservatives. Given this baseline, conservatives were found to be more likely to actually click on cross-cutting content (17%) than liberals (6%) (cf. Messing and Westwood, 2014; Iyengar and Hahn, 2009).

While some researchers feel that simple exposure to diverse information is enough to foster thoughtful consideration of others' opinions which, in turn, may lead to good citizenship behaviors such as voting, Kim and Pasek (2016) counter that diversity-seeking behavior is not always associated with the core value of diversity seeking and that simple exposure is ineffective without this value. They identify four categories of individuals with regard to the relationship between their stated diversity-seeking core values and their real-world practice.

- **Actualizers** hold a diversity-seeking core value and try to achieve it in their behavior.

- **Apathetic** people do not have the diversity-seeking core value and are uninterested in seeking diverse information.

- **Alternatively motivated** do not have a diversity-seeking value but seek out other points of view for purposes unrelated to learning about other perspectives (e.g., building arguments for their own point of view).

- **Aspriationals** hold a diversity-seeking core value but do nothing to realize it.

They found that a plurality of individuals do hold diversity-seeking values, although many of them fail to realize this value in practice. Individuals who held a diversity-seeking core value but who did not actualize this in any practices were nonetheless more knowledgeable about civic matters and more likely to perform positive civic actions like voting. Thus, inculcating diversity-seeking values is critical to good citizenship, but simple exposure to diverse information, or even observed practices of diverse information seeking, is not.

5.2   EQUITY

Habermas conception of the public sphere emphasized equality of access as an important component of healthy deliberation. The same is true for digital deliberation, and, in fact, the issue of equity is amplified to include equitable access to informational, transactional, and collaborative aspects of information technologies. Equity of digital information use is often discussed as a matter of the "digital divide."

The digital divide problem has been recognized as being more than just an issue involving simply access to technology, but also the skills needed to utilize technology (Epstein, 2011) and categorical differences between groups of people (van Dijk, 2005, 2012). Van Dijk (2005, 2012) distinguishes between personal categorical inequalities:

- Age

- Gender

- Race/Ethnicity

- Intelligence

- Personality

- Health

He also identifies the following positional categorical inequalities:

- Labor/Employment status

- Education

- Household

- Nation (developed/developing)

Underlying these categorical differences are various precipitating factors that lead to different levels of involvement with information technologies:

- Temporal (having time to use digital media)

- Material (possession and income)

- Mental (technical ability; motivation)

- Social (having a social network to assist in using digital media)

- Cultural (status and liking of being in the world of digital media)

DiMagio et al. (2004) propose that the digital divide issue be viewed as skill hierarchy. At the base of the hierarchy are skills related to access, further up are technical skills of use for recreational and informational purposes, and further up are skills for using technology for activities that increase social capital. This means that individuals who are in a position to leverage technology for social capital are more likely to participate in civic activities that make a difference such as community organization, voting, and rulemaking (Epstein, Newhart and Vernon, 2014).

Norris (2001) observes that groups that are marginalized in the real world also tend to be marginalized online, suggesting that the "flattening" of access promised by internet technologies continues to be hindered by sociological realities. Barzilai-Nahon (2006) notes that information and networking technologies are often incorrectly perceived as neutral platforms when in fact they are spaces with their own political and social complexities. Online participation by individuals who are capable of utilizing social capital increases their knowledge and influence whereas online participation by individuals who are unable to leverage social and political capital in this way may lead to greater homogeneity in thinking (Brundidge and Rice, 2009).

In the context of political participation, use of information technologies can by hindered by local conditions that are impossible to predict and understand out of context. Farina, Newhart, and Heidt (2012b) describe "situated knowledge" as being important in online deliberation environments because the individuals involved have special, contextually privileged information about impacts, ambiguities, enforceability, causes, unintended consequences, and so on (Epstein, Newhart, and Vernon, 2014). This has an influence on the motivational aspects of the digital divide. Platforms such as Regulation Room (Epstein, Newhart, and Vernon, 2014) are attempts to "strike a balance between broad inclusiveness and informed understanding" (p. 341).

5.3   TRANSPARENCY AND TRUST

Transparency and trust are important factors that are relevant to ICTs and to social media in civic and political situations. Transparency refers to the openness of information and is usually applied to governments themselves and to politicians. Trust derives in part from transparency as far as trust in government and civic institutions goes (Bertot, Jaeger, and Grimes, 2010a; Shim and Eom, 2008, 2009).

West (2004) suggests that exposure to e-government services and information about e-government increases people's sense of the effectiveness of government but does not impact trust. In contrast, Tolbert and Mossberger (2006) found that trust in the processes of government can be increased by use of e-government systems by increasing their exposure to government and positively influencing their sense of government responsiveness.

Welch, Hinnant, and Moon (2005) developed and tested a two-stage model of trust, concluding that use of government websites is positively associated with e-government satisfaction, which in turn is positively associated with trust in government. At the time of this study, the ability of government websites to inform was considered satisfactory but their ability to support interaction and transaction was considered to be unsatisfactory. They distinguish between *process-based* trust, which comes from repeated interactions with e-government systems and is based on how well they work, and *institution-based* trust, which comes from beliefs about how the government handles information about citizens.

Tolbert and Mossberger (2006) describe two conceptualizations of e-government: *entrepreneurial* and *participatory*. In the former, e-government is considered to be a novel form of interaction with citizens. The entrepreneurial approach is judged in terms of its efficiency and responsiveness.

The participatory model of e-government is one that stresses new affordances for citizen involvement. Judgments of the success of e-government systems in this model revolve around increased ability of citizens to be informed, influence others, and communicate with policy makers. Trust is seen as having multiple aspects that derive from these two conceptualizations, including:

- **Responsiveness:** a process-based trust factor that derives from citizens, perception of how efficiently government systems respond to citizen needs and how speedy they are;

- **Accessibility:** a process-based trust factor that derives from citizens' perceptions of whether government systems can be accessed at any time, in any language, and in a manner that matches user needs;

- **Transparency:** an institution-based trust factor that derives from the degree to which governments provide complete and open information; and

- **Responsibility:** An institution-based trust factor involving privacy, equity, and ethical use of information about citizens and their interactions with government.

An important issue when considering differing points of view is the degree to which a person trusts the holder of the alternative viewpoint. Signaling trust is therefore an important goal in sociotechnical systems (Erickson and Kellogg, 2000).

5.4   FAKE NEWS, MISINFORMATION, AND PROPAGANDA

If the press is the Fourth Estate, then the consumption of news in social media contexts is an important aspect of civic engagement. According to the Reuters Institute for the Study of Journalism (Newman, 2017), people in the age range of 18–24 years receive 64% of their news from online sources in contrast to television (24%), print media (6%), and radio (5%). The percentage is 57% for people in the range of 25–35 years and 47% for people in the range of 35–44 years. It is not just that younger people have moved online to consume news from traditional sources, but rather a considerable number of younger people report that they encounter news serendipitously when doing other things online, especially social media.

The structure of social networks often displays a "small-world" character in which important hub nodes connect many peripheral nodes that are not themselves directly connected. The existence of hub nodes means that the distance between any two non-hub, but unconnected points is small (in terms of "hops") since they are likely to be linked through the hub node. In political discussion or follower networks the hub nodes can be media entities or significant, trusted individuals who attract many connections. A desirable characteristic of a small-world network is that information can propagate quickly and broadly. An undesirable quality that has been observed in political discussion on Twitter is that certain hub nodes can act at gatekeepers to filter information (Jürgens, Jungher, and Schoen, 2011).

The internet has been highly disruptive to journalism as a practice, on the one hand opening news reporting up to a broader range of sources (even citizens themselves), but also eroding the authoritative gatekeeping function of respected news sources. The replacement of human editors by algorithms that select "trending" stories for broader dissemination, coupled with easy sharing and notification mechanisms on virtually all social media platforms, has allowed hoaxes, "fake news," and propaganda to spread virally (Nahon and Hemsley, 2013). Newman (2017) finds that people under 35 years of age are highly comfortable with algorithmic selection of news, and receive about 64% of their news from this method in contrast to human editors and recommenders.

Metaxis and Mustafaraj (2010) described a situation in which a tweet about a politician (Martha Coakly, then candidate for U.S. senator from Massachusetts) was generated from multiple fake Twitter accounts. The tweet contained a lie about Ms. Coakly and a link to a website elaborating on that lie. The tweet was subsequently retweeted by 25% of the individuals who saw it (note that the fake Twitter accounts didn't even have followers, but made the tweet visible via hashtags and targeted mentions), including opinion leaders such as journalists. The tweet's influence was then magnified as it began to show up in search results, along with the link. This was one of the earliest identifications and analysis of viral news, which has subsequently become highly problematic. In that light, we should revisit the question posed by Mustafaraj and Metaxis (2017) in a paper revisiting the original finding of Metaxis and Mustafaraj (2010):

> *"[I]n the current context of the omnipresent, web-based, socio-technical systems such as Facebook, Google, and Twitter, what decisions should be made by humans and what by algorithms?"* (p. 239).

News aggregation sites trafficking in propaganda and fake news about U.S. presidential candidates proliferated in 2016, many of them located in other nations. Such sites followed an evolutionary market model that resulted in them becoming more extreme and trending toward pro-Trump and anti-Clinton rhetoric since that attracted the most traffic. Misinformation was planted in social media sites with the goal of spreading virally. Wikileaks engaged in selective leaking of documents in an effort to influence the election. Fear of significant cyber-disruption by Russia against the U.S. election was pervasive, including fear of disruption of electronic voting sites.

Sveningsson (2015) identifies several problematic aspects of new media news consumption by young people.

- **Immediateness:** The fact that news is available as it happens and integrated with other online activities (cf. Coleman Morrison and Anthony (2011) on media convergence).

- **One-sidedness:** Customization of news flow can result in selective exposure. This can both be active, as when a person subscribes to certain sources and rejects others, or passive, as the result of other actions such as choosing friends or following (cf. Mutz and Young, 2011).

- **Fragmentation:** The de-contextualization of information as the result of receiving it on different platforms and in different circumstances (cf. Marchi, 2012, for the alternative perspective that social media adds context).

- **Subjectivity:** Much shared news comes with an opinion or is opinion-based itself.

- **Uncertainty:** The source of news and information often becomes lost.

- **Triviality:** The idea that much news shared by others is "popular" news, and not "real" news. This is not considered problematic by many young people.

Castillo, Mendoza, and Poblete (2011) examined the credibility of news propagated by retweeting in Twitter. The researchers separated news retweets with low believability from those with high believability and then used a supervised classifier to discover features based on characteristics of the message, characteristics of the posters, sentiment and hashtag features, and propagation features. The classifier ultimately reached an 85% threshold for successful discrimination of credible versus non-credible news retweets. Thus it is possible that in the future algorithms will not only select news for us, but also filter itself for trustworthiness.

The internet has become critical at multiple levels of government and society, with social media tools playing ever more important roles. To the degree that networked information systems play a role in civic processes, disruption of those processes becomes a goal of antagonists. For example, Facebook location information can be used to track individuals or understand group patterns of movement, so introducing fake locations into this data is disruptive. In 2016, a Facebook movement arose in conjunction with the Dakota Access Pipeline dispute in the U.S. Facebook users sympathetic to demonstrators were encouraged to "check in," or publicly locate themselves, at the site of a confrontation at the Standing Rock Indian Reservation. Multiple spoofed check-ins were alleged to be disruptive of attempts by authorities to discover who was actually at the site and track their movements. Finally, the manipulation of voters and public opinion in the 2016 U.S. presidential election and subsequent elections in Europe via misleading social media posts customized for viral success is only now being investigated.

5.5   SUMMARY

The fact that so many challenges have arisen in the context of social media and civic participation can be taken as a sign that this area has finally "come of age." Early adopters, perhaps, are usually well intentioned, but all technologies mature to a point where they can be easily appropriated by bad actors and where their negative implications for the broader society become evident. One of the key future tasks of researchers and practitioners in human-centered disciplines will be to monitor, warn, and create solutions to personal and societal implications of social media technologies in the context of the polity.

CHAPTER 6

Epilogue

In this book, the goal has been to take readers through the history of information technology as it applies to civic life, emphasizing emerging social technologies. Since the series focuses on human-centered informatics, the monograph is largely a review of behavioral and sociological work on design, evaluation, impact, and promise of social and ubiquitous technologies on civic engagement.

Because of the pace of change in information technology, keeping this monograph current has been a struggle. For example, as this goes to press the Cambridge Analytica controversy involving Facebook and the 2016 U.S. election is breaking, and an entirely new chapter could be written on privacy and hyperpersonal profiling for political purposes. Despite this, the chapters present enduring information relevant to technology and engagement. The history stands on its own and hopefully serves any reader as a guidepost for exploring the progression of civic information technologies from bulletin boards to smart cities. The theories discussed underlie adoption and use of any new technological innovations and will continue to be helpful as lenses for understanding how novel technologies are adopted and what impacts they will have. The challenges, unfortunately, are also enduring and will certainly continue to be part of the dialog on technology and civic engagement.

The most frustrating part of the monograph will certainly turn out to be the sections on participation and activism. That is because these sections describe what people have actually done with civic technologies to date, and do not anticipate what is to come. As with all treatises on technology, what people are doing with it changes quickly both as new technologies emerge (e.g., Mahoney et al., 2016) and as new practices evolve (Fanti, et al., 2015). So, what is to come?

Most certainly, the dark side of civic technology has only just begun to be explored. Hate speech detection is a new frontier in HCI papers on social media (Badjatiya et al., 2017; Mondal, Silva, and Benevenuto, 2017; Olteanu, Talamadupula, and Varshney, 2017; Warner and Hirschberg, 2012), and this new frontier will figure prominently in future studies of political and civil discourse. Government censorship and social media weaponization will be emerging trends in studies of the digital public commons (Nekrasov, Parks, and Belding, 2017; Wang and Mark, 2013). The issue of biased and false information, fake news, and non-real users is only now becoming topical (Boididou et al., 2017, 2014; Fourney et al., 2017; Narwal et al., 2017; Sethi, 2017) and will continue to grow as autonomous AI chat-targeting systems come online.

Concepts of place and the individual will continue to evolve. For us, space is almost always discussed in a manner that suggests human purpose and agreements about usage. We designate spaces for human activities, e.g., for reading, for sleeping, for thinking; states of mind, e.g., for contemplation, for relaxation, for work; with ownership and boundary signifiers, e.g., public space, my space, restricted space; and with rules, e.g., for adults only, from sunrise until sunset, no alcohol, ticketholders only, pedestrians only. The way cultures organize and designate space is considered by anthropologists and sociologists to be a window into values, practices, social order, and self-image. The way people arrange themselves in a space, what they feel comfortable doing or prohibited from doing, and how they think of themselves differently in different spaces are important clues for understanding the power of space over human experience and behavior. In other words, as far as we are concerned, space is all about us. We fill it with indicators about its purposes and enforce these purposeful interpretations with physical and cultural constraints on activity. Thus, the ever-changing space of digital environments will challenge who we are and what we can do at any given moment (Bauman, 2005; Castells, 2010), even as we take charge of creating our own unique private and public spaces (Foth, Brynskov, and Ojala, 2015a).

Social media platforms take their place as the latest manifestation in a series of sociotechnical innovations designed to enhance civic engagement and political participation. This book is designed to situate social media and new media technologies in the context of prior history and theory in this space and to orient readers to emerging issues and challenges. Social technologies are in their infancy, both in terms of the platforms themselves and in terms of their cultural uptake and evolving uses. We are already witnessing dramatic and swift changes in how social media is used by citizens and polities globally and locally, and they are not all for the best. However, it is reassuring to review the aspirations of visionary sociotechnical theorists and researchers, to assess how far we have come, and to trust that we will ultimately turn these innovations into virtuous public spheres that expand the potential of people to govern themselves in more inclusive, expressive, and positive ways.

Bibliography

Abercrombie, N. and Longhurst, B. J. (1998). *Audiences: A Sociological Theory of Performance and Imagination*. London: Sage Publications. 42

Abroms, L. C. and Lefebvre, R. C. (2009). Obama's wired campaign: Lessons for public health communication. *Journal of Health Communication*, 14(5), 415-423. DOI: 10.1080/10810730903033000. 51

Adamic, L. and Glance, N. (2005). The political blogosphere and the 2004 U.S. election: Divided they blog. *Proceedings of the 3rd ACM International Workshop on Link Discovery*, 36–43. DOI: 10.1145/1134271.1134277. 69, 70

Adler, P. S. and Kwon, S.W. (2002). Social capital: Prospects for a new concept. *The Academy of Management Review*, 27(1), 17–40. DOI: 10.5465/amr.2002.5922314. 37

Agre, P. (2002). Real-time politics: The internet and the political process. *The Information Society*. 18(5), 311–331. DOI: 10.1080/01972240290075174. 69

Al-Ani, B., Mark, G., Chung, J., and Jones, J. (2012). The Egyptian blogosphere: A counter-narrative of the revolution. *Proceedings of CSCW'12: The ACM Conference on Computer Supported Cooperative Work and Social Media*, New York: ACM Press, 17–26. DOI: 10.1145/2145204.2145213. 64, 65, 67

An, J., Quercia, D., and Crowcroft, J. (2014). Partisan sharing: Facebook evidence and societal consequences. *Proceedings of COSN'14: The Second ACM Conference on Online Social Networks*, New York: ACM Press, 13–24. DOI: 10.1145/2660460.2660469. 60

Ancu, M. and Cozma, R. (2009). Myspace politics: Uses and gratifications of befriending candidates. *Journal of Broadcasting and Electronic Media*, 53(4), 567–583. DOI: 10.1080/08838150903333064. 39, 40

Andersen, T. B. (2009). E-government as an anti-corruption strategy. *Information Economics and Policy*, 21(3), 201–210. DOI: 10.1016/j.infoecopol.2008.11.003. 18

Andersen, T. B. and Henriksen, H. Z. (2005). The first leg of e-government research: Domains and application areas 1998-2003. *International Journal of Electronic Government Research*, 1(4), 26–44. DOI: 10.4018/jegr.2005100102. 15

Aral, S., Muchnik, L., and Sundararajan, A. (2009). Distinguishing influence-based contagion from homophily-driven diffusion in dynamic networks. *Proceedings of the National Acad-*

emy of Sciences of the United States of America, 106(51), 21544–21549. DOI: 10.1073/ pnas.0908800106. 44

Arendt, H. (1958). *The Human Condition*. Chicago: The University of Chicago Press. 27

Badjatiya, P., Gupta, S., Gupta, M., and Varma, V. (2017). Deep learning for hate speech detection in tweets. *Proceedings of the 26th International Conference on World Wide Web*, 759–760. DOI: 10.1145/3041021.3054223. 79

Bakker, T.P. and de Vreese C.H. (2011). Good news for the future? Young people, internet use, and political participation. *Communication Research*, 38(4), 451–470. DOI: 10.1177/0093650210381738. 40

Bakshy, E., Messing, S., and Adamic, L. A. (2015). Exposure to ideologically diverse news and opinion on Facebook. *Science*, 348(6239), 1130–1132. DOI: 10.1126/science.aaa1160. 71

Barber, B. R., Mattson, K., and Peterson, J. (1997). *The State of 'Electronically Enhanced Democracy': A Survey of the Internet*. New Brunswick, NJ: Walt Whitman Center. 48

Barocas, S. (2012). The price of precision: Voter microtargeting and its potential harms to the democratic process. *Proceedings of PLEAD: The First Edition Workshop on Politics, Elections, and Data*. New York: ACM Press, 31–36. DOI: 10.1145/2389661.2389671. 54

Barzilai-Nahon, K. (2006). Gaps and bits: Conceptualizing measurements for digital divide/s. *The Information Society*, 22(5), 269–278. DOI: 10.1080/01972240600903953. 73

Bauman, Z. (2005). *Liquid Life*. Cambridge: Polity Press. 80

Baumgartner, J. C. and Morris, J. S. (2010). MyFaceTube politics: Social networking websites and political engagement of young adults. *Social Science Computer Review*, 28(1), 24–44. DOI: 10.1177/0894439309334325. 49, 55

Belanger, F. and Carter, L. (2012). Digitizing government interactions with constituents: An historical review of e-government research in information systems. *Journal of the Association of Information Systems*, 13(5). Available at: http://aisel.aisnet.org/jais/vol13/iss5/1. DOI: 10.17705/1jais.00295. 15

Benkler, Y. (2006). *The Wealth of Networks*. New Haven, CT: Yale University Press. 2, 3

Bennett, W. L. (2007). Civic learning in changing democracies: Challenges for citizenship and civic education. In P. Dahlgren (Ed.), *Young Citizens and New Media: Learning Democratic Engagement* (pp. 59–77). New York: Routledge. 50

Bennett, W. L. (2008). Changing citizenship in the digital age. In W. L. Bennett (Ed.), *Civic Life Online* (pp. 1–24). Cambridge, MA: MIT Press. 50

Bennett, W. L. and Segerberg, A. (2011). Digital media and the personalization of collective action: Social technology and the organization of protests against the global economic crisis. *Information, Communication and Society*, 14(6), 770–799. DOI: 10.1080/1369118X.2011.579141. 51

Bennett, W. L., Wells, C., and Freelon, D. (2011). Communicating civic engagement: Contrasting models of citizenship in the youth web sphere. *Journal of Communication*, 61(5), 835–856. DOI: 10.1111/j.1460-2466.2011.01588.x. 50, 51

Benoit, W. L., Hansen, G. J., and Verser, R. M. (2003). A meta-analysis of the effects of viewing U.S. presidential debates. *Communication Monographs*, 70, 335-35. DOI: 10.1080/0363775032000179133. 62

Beraldo, D. and Galan-Paez, J. (2013). The #occupy network on twitter and the challenges to social movements theory and research. *International Journal of Electronic Governance*, 6(4), 319–341. DOI: 10.1504/IJEG.2013.060646. 43

Bertot, J. C., Gorhamn U., Jaeger, P. T., and Choi, H. (2014). Big data, open government and e-government: Issues policies and recommendations. *Information Polity*, 19(1), 5-16. 18

Bertot, J. C., Jaeger, P. T., and Grimes, J. (2010). Using ICTs to create a culture of transparency: E-government and social media as openness and anti-corruption tools for societies. *Government Information Quarterly*, 27(3), 264–271. DOI: 10.1016/j.giq.2010.03.001. 18, 19, 74

Bertot, J. C., Jaeger, P. T., Munson, S., and Glaisyer, T. (2010). Engaging the public in open government: The policy and government application of social media technology for government transparency. *IEEE Computer*, 43(11), 53–59. DOI: 10.1109/MC.2010.325. 19

Bertot, J. C., Jaeger, P. T., and Hanse, D. (2012). The impact of polices on government social media usage: Issues, challenges, and recommendations. *Government Information Quarterly*, 29(1), 30–40. DOI: 10.1016/j.giq.2011.04.004. 19

Bimber, B. (1999). The internet and citizen communication with government: Does the medium matter? *Political Communication*, 16(4), 409–428. DOI: 10.1080/105846099198569.

Bimber, B. (2000). The study of information technology and civic engagement. *Political Communication*, 17(4), 329–333. DOI: 10.1080/10584600050178924. 17

Bimber, B. (2001). Information and political engagement in America: The search for effects of information technology at the individual level. *Political Research Quarterly*, 54(1), 53–67. DOI: 10.1177/106591290105400103. 49

Bimber, B. and Copeland, L. (2013). Digital media and traditional political participation over time in the U.S. *Journal of Information Technology and Politics*, 10(2), 125–137. DOI: 10.1080/19331681.2013.769925. 49

Bimber, B. and Davis, R. (2003). *Campaigning Online: The Internet in U.S. Elections*. Oxford: Oxford University Press. 49, 70

Bode, L. (2012). Facebooking it to the Polls: A study in online social networking and political behavior. *Journal of Information Technology and Politics*, 9(4), 352-369. DOI: 10.1080/19331681.2012.709045. 50

Bode, L. (2015). Political news in the news feed: Learning politics from social media. *Mass Communication and Society*, 19(1), 24–48. DOI: 10.1080/15205436.2015.1045149. 60

Boeder, P. (2005). Habermas' heritage: The future of the public sphere in the network society. *First Monday*, 10(9), September. DOI: 10.5210/fm.v10i9.1280. 2

Boehner, K. and DiSalvo, C. (2016). Data, design and civics: An exploratory study of civic tech. *Proceedings of CHI'16: The ACM Conference on Human Factors in Computing Systems*. New York: ACM, 2970–2981. DOI: 10.1145/2858036.2858326. 20, 22

Boididou, C., Papadopoulos, S., Apostolidis, L., and Kompatsiaris, Y. (2017). Learning to detect misleading content on Twitter. *ICMR'17: Proceedings of the ACM International Conference on Multimedia Retrieval*. New York: ACM Press, 278–286. DOI: 10.1145/3078971.3078979. 79

Boididou, C., Papadopoulos, S., Kompatsiaris, Y., Schifferes, S., and Newman, N. (2014). Challenges of computational verification in social multimedia. *WWW'14: Proceedings of the 23rd International Conference on World Wide Web*. New York: ACM Press, 743–748. DOI: 10.1145/2567948.2579323. 79

Bond, R. M., Fariss, C. J., Jones, J. J., Kramer, A. D. I., Marlow, C., Settle, J. E., and Fowler, J. H. (2012). A 61-million-person experiment in social influence and political mobilization. *Nature*, 489, 295–298. DOI: 10.1038/nature11421. 60

Bonsón, E., Torres, L., Royo, S., and Flores, F. (2012). Local e-government 2.0: Social media and corporate transparency in municipalities. *Government Information Quarterly*, 29(2), 123–132. DOI: 10.1038/nature11421. 19

Booten, K. (2016). Hashtag drift: Tracing the evolving uses of political hashtags over time. *CHI'16: Proceedings of the 2016 ACM Conference on Human Factors in Computing Systems*. New York: ACM, 2401–2405. DOI: /10.1145/2858036.2858398. 51

Boulianne, S. (2009). Does Internet use affect engagement? A meta-analysis of research. *Political Communication*, 26, 193–211. DOI:10.1080/10584600902854363. 3, 50

Boulianne, S. (2015a). Online news, civic awareness, and engagement in civic and political life. *New Media and Society*, 18(9), 1840–1856. DOI: 10.1177/1461444815616222. 49

Boulianne, S.(2015b). Social media use and participation: a meta-analysis of current research. *Information, Communication and Society*, 18 (5), 524–538. DOI: 10.1080/1369118X.2015.1008542.

Boutet, A., Kim, H., and Yoneki, E. (2012). What's in Twitter: I know what parties are popular and who you are supporting now! *Proceedings of the 2012 International Conference on Advances in Social Networks Analysis and Mining*, New York:ACM Press, 132–129. DOI: 10.1109/ASONAM.2012.32. 70

boyd, d. (2008). None of this is real. In J. Karaganis, *Structures of Participation in Digital Culture*. (pp. 132-157). New York: Social Science Research Council. 37

boyd, d. (2010). Social network sites as networked publics: Affordances, dynamics, and implications. In Z. Papacharissi (Ed.), *A Networked Self: Identity, Xommunity, and Xulture on Social Network Sites* (pp. 39–58). New York: Routledge. 37, 38

Boynton, G. R. and Richardson, G. W. (2015). Agenda setting in the twenty-first century. *New Media and Society*, 18(9), 1916–1934. DOI: 10.1177/1461444815616226. 54

Brainard, L. A. and McNutt, J. G. (2010). Virtual government-citizen relations. Informational, transactional, or collaborative? *Administration and Society*, 42(7), 836–858. DOI: 10.1177/0095399710386308. 19

Brake, D. R. (2012). Who do they think they're talking to? Framings of the audience by social media users. *International Journal of Communication*, 6, 1056–1076. 37, 38

Braman, S. (1995). Policy for the net and the internet. *Annual Review of Information Science and Technology (ARIST)*, 30, 5–75. 15

Brundidge, J. (2010). Encountering "Difference" in the contemporary public sphere: The contribution of the Internet to the heterogeneity of political discussion networks. *Journal of Communication*, 60, 680–700. DOI: 10.1111/j.1460-2466.2010.01509.x. 71

Brundidge, J. and Rice, R. E. (2009). Political engagement online: Do the information rich get richer and the like-minded more similar? In A. Chadwick, and P. N. Howard (Eds.), *Routledge Handbook of Internet Politics* (pp. 144–156). New York: Taylor and Francis. 74

Bryant, J. and Miron, D. (2004). Theory and research in mass communication. *Journal of Communication*, 54(4), 662–704. DOI: 10.1111/j.1460-2466.2004.tb02650.x. 41

Bucy, E. P. and Gregson, K. S. (2001). Media participation: A legitimizing mechanism of mass democracy. *New Media and Society*, 3(3), 357–380. DOI: 10.1177/1461444801003003006. 50, 58

Burns, A. and Eltham, B. (2009). Twitter free Iran: An evaluation of Twitter's role in public diplomacy and information operations in Iran's 2009 Election Crisis. In F. Papandrea and M. Armstrong (Eds.), *Record of the Communications Policy and Research Forum 2009* (pp. 298–310), Sydney: Network Insight Institute. 63

Cameron, J. and Geidner, N. (2014). Something old, something new, something borrowed from something blue: Experiments on dual viewing TV and Twitter. *Journal of Broadcasting and Electronic Media* 58(3), 400–419. DOI: 10.1080/08838151.2014.935852. 62

Caren, N. and Gaby, S. (2011). Occupy online: Facebook and the spread of Occupy Wall Street. *Social Science Research Network*. SSRN. DOI: 10.2139/ssrn.1943168. 7

Carpentier, N. (2011). *Media and Participation. A Site of Ideological-democratic Struggle*. Bristol: Intellect. DOI: 10.26530/OAPEN_606390. 42

Carpentier, N. (2015). Differentiating between access, interaction and participation. *Conjunctions: Transdisciplinary Journal of Cultural Participation*, 2(2), DOI: 10.7146/tjcp.v2i2.22844. 42

Carroll, J. M. (2005). The Blacksburg electronic village: A study in community computing. In P. van den Besselaar and S. Koizumi (Eds.), *Digital Cities 2003, Lecture Notes in Computer Science*, 3081, 43–65. DOI: 10.1007/11407546_3. 14

Carroll, J. M., Hoffman, B., Han, K., and Rosson, M. B. (2015). Reviving community network: Hyperlocality and suprathresholding in Web 2.0 designs. *Personal and Ubiquitous Computing*, 19, 477–491. DOI: 10.1007/s00779-014-0831-y. 23, 24

Carroll, J. M., Rosson, M. B., Isenhour, P. L., Ganoe, C. H., Dunlap, D., Fogarty, J., Schafer, W., and Van Metre, C. (2001). Designing our town: MOOsburg. *International Journal of Human-Computer Studies*, 54, 725–751. DOI: 10.1006/ijhc.2000.0438. 14

Carroll, J. M. and Rosson, M. B. (1996). Developing the Blacksburg electronic village. *Communications of the ACM*, 39(12), December, 69-74. DOI: 10.1145/240483.240498. 14

Carroll, J. M., Rosson, M. B., Cohill, A. M., and Schorger, J. R. (1995). Building a history of the Blacksburg Electronic Village. In P*roceedings of the 1st Conference on Designing Interactive Systems: Processes, Practices, Methods, & Techniques (DIS '95)*, New York: ACM, 1–6. DOI: 10.1145/225434.225435.14

Castells, M. (1996). *The Rise of the Network Society (The Information Age: Economy, Society, and Culture, Volume 1)*. Malden, MA: Blackwell. 17

Castells, M. (2001). *The Internet Galaxy. Reflections on the Internet, Business, and Society*. Oxford, UK: Oxford University Press. DOI: 10.1007/978-3-322-89613-1. 37

Castells, M. (2007). Communication, power and counter-power in the network society. *International Journal of Communication*, 1(1), 238–66. 64

Castells, M. (2009). *Communication Power*. Oxford: Oxford University Press. 2, 64

Castells, M. (2010). *The Power of Identity (The Information Age: Economy, Society, and Culture, Volume II)*. Malden, MA: Blackwell. 80

Castillo, C., Mendoza, M., and Poblete, B. (2011). Information credibility on Twitter. *Proceedings of WWW2011*, 675–684. DOI: 10.1145/1963405.1963500. 77

Ceron, A. (2015). Internet, news and political trust: The difference between social media and online media outlets. *Journal of Computer-Mediated Communication*, 20(5), 487–503. DOI: 10.1111/jcc4.12129. 42

Ceron, A., Curini, L., and Iacus, S. M. (2016). First- and second-level agenda setting in the Twittersphere: An application to the Italian political debate. *Journal of Information Technology and Politics*, 13(2), 159–174. DOI: 10.1080/19331681.2016.1160266. 41

Cho, J., Shah, D. V., McLeod, J. M., Scholl, R. M., and Gotlieb, M. R. (2009). Campaigns, reflection, and deliberation: Advancing an O-S-R-O-R model of communication effects. *Communication Theory*, 19(1), 66–88. DOI: 10.1111/j.1468-2885.2008.01333.x. 49

Chong, D. and Druckman, J. N. (2007). Framing theory. *Annual Review of Political Science*, 10(1), 103–126. DOI: 10.1146/annurev.polisci.10.072805.103054. 41

Chun, S. A., Shulman, S., Sandoval, R., and Hovy, E. (2010). Government 2.0: Making connections between citizens, data and government. *Information Polity*, 15(1-2), 1–9. 19

Church, S. H. (2010). YouTube politics: YouChoose and leadership rhetoric during the 2008 election. *Journal of Information Technology and Politics*, 7(2-3), 124–142. DOI: 10.1080/19331681003748933. 51

Cogburn, D. L. and Espinoza-Vasquez, F. K. (2011). From networked nominee to networked nation: Examining the impact of Web 2.0 and social media on political participation and civic engagement in the 2008 Obama campaign. *Journal of Political Marketing*, 10(1–2), 189-213. DOI: 10.1080/15377857.2011.540224. 50, 51

Coleman, J. S. (1988). Social capital in the creation of human capital. *The American Journal of Sociology*, 94, S95–S120. DOI: 10.1086/228943. 35

Coleman, J. S. (1990). *Foundations of Social Theory*. Cambridge, MA: Harvard University Press. 35

Coleman, S. (2007). From big brother to big brother: Two faces of interactive engagement. In P. Dahlgren (Ed.), Young citizens and new media: Learning democratic engagement. NewYork: Routledge. 50

Coleman, S. (2008). Doing IT for themselves: Management versus autonomy in youth e-citizenship. In W. L. Bennett (Ed.), *Civic Life Online: Learning how Digital Media can Engage Youth* (pp. 189–206). Cambridge, MA: MIT Press. 50

Coleman, S., Morrison, D. E., and Anthony, S. (2011). A constructivist study of trust in the news. *Journalism Studies*, 13, 37–53. DOI: 10.1080/1461670X.2011.592353. 70, 76

Colleoni, E., Rozza, A., and Arvidsson, A. (2014), Echo chamber or public sphere? Predicting political orientation and measuring political homophily in Twitter using big data. *Journal of Communication*, 64, 317–332. DOI: 10.1111/jcom.12084. 69

Conover, M. D., Ratkiewicz, J., Francisco, M., Goncalves, B., Menczer, F., and Flammini, A. (2011). Political polarization on Twitter. *Proceedings of the Fifth International AAAI Conference on Weblogs and Social Media.* 70

Conway, B. A., Kenski, K., and Wang, D. (2013). Twitter use by presidential primary candidates during the 2012 campaign. *American Behavioral Scientist*, 57(11), 1596–1610. DOI: 10.1177/0002764213489014. 51, 55

Conway, B. A., Kenski, K., and Wang, D. (2015). The rise of Twitter in the political campaign: Searching for intermedia agenda-setting effects in the presidential primary. *Journal of Computer-Mediated Communication*, 20(4), 363–380. DOI:10.1111/jcc4.12124. 42, 51, 54

Cook, E. C. and Teasley, S. D. (2011). Beyond promotion and protection: Creators, audiences and common ground in user-generated media. *Proceedings of the 2011 iConference.* New York: ACM Press, 41–47. DOI: 10.1145/1940761.1940767. 38

Cooper, W. E. (1992). William James's theory of the self. *Monist*, 75(4), 504. DOI: 10.5840/monist199275425. 38

Cornfield, M. (2004). *Politics Moves Online: Campaigning and the Internet.* New York: The Century Foundation Press. 52

Cornfield, M., Carson, J., Kalis, A., and Simon, E. (2005). Buzz, blogs, and beyond: The Internet and the national discourse in the fall of 2004. Pew Internet and American Life Project. 41

Cosley, D., Huttenlocher, D. P., Kleinberg, J. M., Lan, X., and Suri S. (2010). Sequential influence models in social networks. *Proceedings of the 4th International Conference on Weblogs and Social Media.* 44

Crane, R. and Sornette D. (2008). Robust dynamic classes revealed by measuring the response function of a social system. *Proceedings of the National Academy of Sciences of the United States of America*, 105(41), 15649–15653. DOI: 10.1073/pnas.0803685105. 44

Cranshaw, J., Schwartz, R., Hong, J. I., and Sadeh, N. (2012). The Livehoods project: Utilizing social media to understand the dynamics of a city. *Proceedings of the Sixth International AAAI Conference on Weblogs and Social Media*. AAAI, 58–65. 23

Crivellaro, C., Comber, R., Bowers, J., Wright, P. C., and Olivier, P. (2014). A pool of dreams: Facebook, politics and the emergence of a social movement. *Proceedings of CHI'14: ACM Conference on Human Factors in Computing Systems*. New York: ACM, 3573–3582. DOI: 10.1145/2556288.2557100. 62

Cuninghame, P. (2010). Autonomism as a global social movement. *WorkingUSA: The Journal of Labor and Society*, 13(4), 451-464. DOI: 10.1111/j.1743-4580.2010.00305.x. 35

Dahlberg, L. (2001). Computer-mediated communication and the public sphere: A critical analysis. *Journal of Computer Mediated Communication*, 7(1). DOI: 10.1111/j.1083-6101.2001. tb00137.x. 2

Dahlberg, L. (2004). The Habermasian public sphere: A specification of the idealized conditions of democratic communication. *Studies in Social and Political Thought*, 10, 2–18. 28

Dahlberg, L. (2010). Cyber-libertarianism 2.0: A discourse theory/critical political economy exam-ination. *Cultural Politics*, 6(3), 331–356. DOI: 10.2752/175174310X12750685679753. 35

Dahlberg, L. (2011). Re-constructing digital democracy: An outline of four 'positions.' *New Media and Society*, 13(6), 855 872. DOI: 10.1177/1461444810389569. 34

Dahlgren, P. (2005). The Internet, public spheres, and political communication: Dispersion and de-liberation. *Political Communication*, 22(2), 147–162. DOI: 10.1080/10584600590933160. 2, 30

Dahlgren, P. (2009). *Media and Political Engagement*. New York: Cambridge University Press. 2, 30

Dahlgren, P. (2016). Civic engagement. *The International Encyclopedia of Political Communication*. 119–128. DOI: 10.1002/9781118541555.wbiepc061. 2

Dalrymple, K. E. and Scheufele, D. A. (2007). Finally informing the electorate? How the Internet got people thinking about presidential politics in 2004. *Harvard International Journal of Press/Politics*, 12(3), 96–111. DOI: 10.1177/1081180X07302881. 50

Davies, T. and Frank, M. (2013). 'There's no such thing as raw data': Exploring the socio-technical life of a government dataset. *Proceedings of the 5th Annual ACM Web Science Conference (WebSci '13)*. ACM, New York, 75-78. DOI=10.1145/2464464.2464472. 19

Davis, R. (1999). *The Web of Politics: The Internet's Impact on the American Political System*. New York: Oxford University Press. 51, 70Dean, J. (2003). Why the net is not a public sphere. *Con-*

stellations: An International Journal of Critical and Democratic Theory, 10(1), 95–112. DOI: 10.1111/1467-8675.00315. 28, 33

Delli Carpini, M. X. (2000). Gen.com: Youth, civic engagement, and the new information environment. *Political Communication*, 17(4), 341–349. DOI: 10.1080/10584600050178942. 3

Delli Carpini, M. X., Cook, F. L., and Jacobs, L. R. (2004). Participation, and citizen engagement: A review of the empirical literature. *Annual Review of Political Science*, 7, 315–344. DOI: 10.1146/annurev.polisci.7.121003.091630. 69

DePaula, N. and Dincelli, E. (2016). An empirical analysis of local government social media communication: Models of e-government interactivity and public relations. *Proceedings of the 17th International Digital Government Research Conference on Digital Government Research (dg.o '16)*, Yushim Kim and Monica Liu (Eds.), New York: ACM, 348–356. DOI: 10.1145/2912160.2912174. 8

Desanctis, G. and Poole, M. S. (1994). Capturing the complexity in advanced technology use: Adaptive structuration theory. *Organization Science*, 5, p. 132. DOI: 10.1287/orsc.5.2.121. 42

Devlin, L. P. (2005). Contrasts in presidential campaign commercials of 2004. *American Behavioural Scientist*, 49(2), 279–313. DOI: 10.1177/0002764205279414. 52

De Waal, M. (2014). *The City as Interface: How New Media are Changing the City*. The Netherlands: nai010 publishers. 22

DiMaggio, P., Hargittai, E., Celeste, C., and Shafer, S. (2004). Digital inequality: From unequal access to differentiated use. In K. M. Neckerman (Ed.), *Social Inequality* (pp. 355–400). New York: Russell Sage Foundation. 3, 73

Dimitrova, D. V., Shehata, A., Strömbäck, J., and Nord, L. W. (2014). The effects of digital media on political knowledge and participation in election campaigns: Evidence from panel data. *Communication Research*, 41(1), 95–118. DOI: 10.1177/0093650211426004. 49, 50

Dimond, J. P., Dye, M., Larose, D., and Bruckman, A. S. (2013). Hollaback!: the role of storytelling online in a social movement organization. *Proceedings of CSCW'13: The 2013 ACM Conference on Computer Supported Cooperative Work*, New York: ACM Press, 477–490. DOI: 10.1145/2441776.2441831. 67

Dincelli, E., Hong, Y., and DePaula, N. (2016). Information diffusion and opinion change during the gezi park protests: Homophily or social influence? *Proceedings of the Association for*

Information Science and Technology, 53(1), 1–5. DOI: 10.1002/pra2.2016.14505301109. 7

Doan, A., Ramakrishnan, R., and Halevy, A. Y. (2011). Crowdsourcing systems on the World-Wide Web. *Communications of the ACM*, 54, 4 (Apr.), 86–96. DOI: 10.1145/1924421.1924442. 19

Donath, J. and boyd, d. (2004). Public displays of connection. *BT Technology Journal*, 22(4), 71–82. DOI: 10.1023/B:BTTJ.0000047585.06264.cc. 5

Dostie-Goulet, E. (2009). Social networks and the development of political interest. *Journal of Youth Studies*, 12(4), 405–421. DOI: 10.1080/13676260902866512. 57

Douglas, S., Maruyama, M., Semaan, B., and Robertson, S. P. (2014). Politics and young adults: the effects of Facebook on candidate evaluation. *Proceedings of the 15th Annual International Conference on Digital Government Research* (dg.o '14). ACM, New York, NY, USA, 196–204. DOI: 10.1145/2612733.2612754. 50, 56, 57

Dourish, P. (2010). HCI and Environmental Sustainability: The Politics of Design and the Design of Politics. *Proceedings of DIS 2010: The 8th ACM Conference on Designing Interactive Systems.* New York: ACM, 1–10. DOI: 10.1145/1858171.1858173.63

Druckman, J. N., Kifer, M. J., and Parkin, M. (2009). Campaign communications in US congressional elections. *American Political Science Review*, 103(3), 343–366. DOI: 10.1017/S0003055409990037. 52

Dryzek, J. S. (1990). *Discursive Democracy: Politics, Policy, and Political Science.* Cambridge: Cambridge University Press. 2

Dryzek, J. S. (2000). *Deliberative Democracy and Beyond: Liberals, Critics, Contestations.* Oxford: Oxford University Press. 2

Ekström, M. and Östman, J. (2013). Information, interaction, and creative production: The effects of three forms of internet use on youth democratic engagement. *Communication Research*, 42(6), 796–818. DOI: 10.1177/0093650213476295. 40

Ellison, N. B., Steinfield, C., and Lampe, C. (2007). The benefits of Facebook "friends:" Social capital and college students' use of online social network sites. *Journal of Computer-Mediated Communication*, 12(4), 1–29. DOI: 10.1111/j.1083-6101.2007.00367.x. 5, 40

Epstein, D. (2011). The analog history of the "digital divide". In D. W. Park, N. W. Jankowski, and S. Jones (Eds.), *The Long History of New Media: Technology, Historiography and Contextualizing Newness* (pp. 127–144). New York: Peter Lang Publishing. 72

Epstein, D., Newhart, M. and Vernon, R. (2014). Not by technology alone: The "analog" aspects of online public engagement in policymaking. *Government Information Quarterly*, 31, 337–344. DOI: 10.1016/j.giq.2014.01.001. 73, 74

Erickson, T. and Kellogg, W. A. (2000). Social translucence. *ACM Transactions on Computer-Human Interaction*, 7(1), 59-83. DOI: 10.1145/344949.345004. 75

European Commission (2013). *Open Data Policy*. Available at: https://ec.europa.eu/digital-single-market/en/open-data. 18

Evans, H. K., Cordova, V., and Sipole, S (2014). Twitter-style: An analysis of how House candidates used Twitter in their 2012 campaigns. *PS: Political Science and Politics*, 47(2), pp 454–461. DOI: 10.1017/S1049096514000389. 52

Fanti, G., Kairouz, P., Oh, S., and Viswanath, P. (2015). Spy vs. spy: Rumor source obfuscation. *Proceedings of SIGMETRICS'15: ACM International Conference on Measurement and Modeling of Computer Systems*, New York: ACM, 271–284. DOI: 10.1145/2745844.2745866. 79

Farina, C. R., Epstein, D., Heidt, J., and Newhart, M. J. (2012a). Knowledge in the people: Rethinking "value" in public rulemaking participation. *Wake Forest Law Review*, 47(5), 1185–1241.

Farina, C. R., Newhart, M. J., and Heidt, J. B. (2012b). Rulemaking vs. democracy: Judging and nudging public participation that counts. *Michigan Journal of Environmental and Administrative Law*, 2(1), 123–172. 74

Farnham, S. D. and Churchill, E. F. (2011). Faceted identity, faceted lives: social and technical issues with being yourself online. *Proceedings CSCW'11: ACM Conference on Computer Supported Cooperative Work*, New York: ACM Press, 359–368. DOI: 10.1145/1958824.1958880. 38

Farrington. C. and Pine, E. (1996). Community memory: A case study in community communication. In P. Agre and D. Schuler (Eds.), *Reinventing Technology, Rediscovering Community*. Albex. 13

Ferro, E., Loukis, E. N., Charalabidis, Y., and Osella, M. (2013). Policy making 2.0: From theory to practice. *Government Information Quarterly* 30(4), 359–368. DOI: 10.1016/j.giq.2013.05.018. 19

Foley, M. W. and Edwards, B. (1997). Escape from politics? Social theory and the social capital debate. *American Behavioral Scientist*, 40(5), 550–561. DOI: 10.1177/0002764297040005002. 36

Foot, K. and Schneider, S. M. (2002). Online action in campaign 2000: An exploratory analysis of the U.S. political web sphere. *Journal of Broadcasting and Electronic Media*, 46(2), 222–244. DOI: 10.1207/s15506878jobem4602_4. 47, 48

Foot, K. and Schneider, K. A. (2006). *Web Campaigning*. Cambridge, MA: MIT Press. 48

Foth, M. (Ed.) (2009). *Handbook of Research on Urban Informatics: The Practice and Promise of the Real-Time City*. Hershey, PA: IGI Global. DOI: 10.4018/978-1-60566-152-0. 22

Foth, M. (2017). Lessons from urban guerrilla placemaking for smart city commons. *Proceedings of C&T'17: 8th International Conference on Communities and Technologies*. New York: ACM Press, 32–35. DOI: 10.1145/3083671.3083707. 22

Foth, M., Choi, J. H., and Satchell, C. (2011). Urban informatics. *Proceedings CSCW'11: ACM Conference on Computer Supported Cooperative Work*. New York: ACM Press, 1–8. DOI: 10.1145/1958824.1958826. 22

Foth, M., Brynskov, M., and Ojala, T. (2015a). *Citizen's Right to the Digital City*. Springer. DOI: 10.1007/978-981-287-919-6. 80

Foth, M., Tomitsch, M., Satchell, C., and Haeusler, M. H. (2015b). From users to citizens: Some thoughts on designing for polity and civics. *Proceedings of OzCHI'15: Annual Meeting of the Australian Special Interest Group for Computer-Human Interaction*. New York: ACM Press, 623–633. DOI: 10.1145/2838739.2838769. 20, 22

Fountain, J. (2002). Toward a theory of federal bureaucracy for the twenty-first century. In E.C. Kamarck and J.S. Nye Jr. (Eds.), *Governance.com: Democracy in the Information Age*. 117–140. 15

Fourney, A., Racz, M. Z., Ranade, G., Mobius, M., and Horvitz, E. (2017). Geographic and temporal trends in fake news consumption during the 2016 US presidential election. *Proceedings of CIKM'17: ACM Conference on Information and Knowledge Management*. New York: ACM Press, 2071-2074. DOI: 10.1145/3132847.3133147. 79

Francoli, M. (2011). What makes governments 'open'? *Journal of Democracy and Open Government*, 3(2), 152–165. 18

Fraser, N. (1990). Rethinking the public sphere: A contribution to the critique of actually existing democracy, *Social Text*, 25/26, 56–80. DOI: 10.2307/466240. 29, 63

Fraser, M. and Dutta, S. (2008). Barack Obama and the Facebook election. *US News and World Report* (November 19). 51

Freelon, D. G. (2010). Analyzing online political discussion using three models of democratic communication. *New Media and Society*, 12(7), 1172–1190. DOI: 10.1177/1461444809357927. 35

Galston, W. A. (2003). If political fragmentation is the problem, is the Internet the solution? In D. M. Anderson and M. Cornfield (Eds.), *The Civic Web: Online Politics and Democratic Values* (pp. 35–44). Lanham, MD: Rowman and Littlefield. 70

Garrett. R. (2009). Echo chambers online?: Politically motivated selective exposure among Internet news users. *Journal of Computer-Mediated Communication*, 14(2), 265–285. DOI: 10.1111/j.1083-6101.2009.01440.x. 70

Gerhards, J. and Shäfer, M. S. (2010). Is the internet a better public sphere? Comparing old and new media in the USA and Germany. *New Media and Society*, 12(1), 143–160. DOI: 10.1177/1461444809341444. 3

Gertner, J. (2004). The very, very personal is the political. *The New York Times Magazine* (February 15). 54

Giddens, A. (1984). *The Constitution of Society: Outline of the Theory of Structure.* Berkeley, CA: University of California Press. 42

Gil de Zúñiga, H., Copeland, H., and Bimber, B. (2013). Political consumerism: Civic engagement and the social media connection. *New Media and Society*, 16(3), 488–506. DOI: 10.1177/1461444813487960. 50

Gil de Zúñiga, H., Jung, N., and Valenzuela, S. (2012). Social media use for news and individuals' social capital, civic engagement and political participation. *Journal of Computer-Mediated Communication*, 17(3), 319–336. DOI: 10.1111/j.1083-6101.2012.01574.x. 49, 50

Gil de Zúñiga, H., Puig-I-Abril, E., and Rojas, H. (2009). Weblogs, traditional sources online and political participation: An assessment of how the internet is changing the political environment. *New Media and Society*, 11(4), 553–574. DOI: 10.1177/1461444809102960. 60

Gil de Zúñiga, H., Valenzuela, S., and Weeks, B. E. (2016). Motivations for political discussion: Antecedents and consequences on civic engagement. *Human Communication Research*, 42(4). 39

Gilbert, E., Bergstrom, T., and Karahalios, K. (2009). Blogs are echo chambers: Blogs are echo chambers. *Proceedings of the 42nd Hawaii International Conference on System Sciences*, Washington, DC: IEEE Computer Society, 1–10. 69

Gitelman, L. (2013). *"Raw Data" Is an Oxymoron.* The MIT Press. 19

Goffman, E. (1990). *The Presentation of Self in Everyday Life.* London: Penguin Books. 37, 43

Golbeck, J., Grimes, J. M. and Rogers, A. (2010). Twitter use by the U.S. Congress. *Journal of the American Society for Information Science and Technology*, 61(8), 1612–1621. DOI: 10.1002/asi.21344. 52, 53

Goldman, S. K. and Mutz, D. C. (2011). The friendly media phenomenon: A cross-national analysis of cross-cutting exposure. *Political Communication*, 28(1), 42–66. DOI: 10.1080/10584609.2010.544280. 60

Gomes, A. and Soares, D. (2014). Open government data initiatives in Europe: northern versus southern countries analysis. *ICEGOV'14: Proceedings of the 8th International Conference on Theory and Practice of Electronic Governance*. New York: ACM, 342–350. DOI: 10.1145/2691195.2691246. 18

Gordon, E., Baldwin-Philippi, J., and Balestra, M. (2013) Why we engage: How theories of human behavior contribute to our understanding of civic engagement in a digital era. Berkman Center Research Publication No. 21. (October 22, 2013). DOI: 10.2139/ssrn.2343762. 4

Gorkovenko, K. and Taylor, N. (2016). Politics at home: second screen behaviours and Motivations during TV debates. *NordiCHI'16: Proceedings of the 9th Nordic Conference on Human-Computer Interaction*. New York: ACM, Article 22, 10 pages. DOI: 10.1145/2971485.2971514. 61

Gottfried, J. and Shearer, A. (2016). News use across social media platforms 2016. Pew Research Center, May. Avilable at: http://www.journalism.org/2016/05/26/news-use-across-social-media-platforms-2016/. 8

Graham, T., Broersma, M., Hazelhoff, K., and van't Haar, G. (2013). Between broadcasting political messages and interacting with voters: the use of Twitter during the 2010 UK general election campaign. *Information, Communication and Society*, 16(5), 692–716. DOI: 10.1080/1369118X.2013.785581. 48

Granka, L. (2009). Inferring the public agenda from implicit query data. In *UIIR-2009: Understanding the User-Logging and Interpreting User Interactions in Informal Search and Retrieval*, 28–31. 56

Granka, L. (2013). Using online search traffic to predict US presidential elections. *PS: Political Science and Politics*, 46(2), 271-279. DOI: S1049096513000292. 56

Granovetter, M. S. (1973). The strength of weak ties. *American Journal of Sociology*, 78(6), 1360–1380. DOI: 10.1086/225469. 36

Granovetter, M. S. (1982). The strength of weak ties: A network theory revisited. In P. V. Marsden and N. Lin (Eds.), *Social Structure and Network Analysis*, 105-130. Beverly Hills, CA: Sage. 36

Greenwood, S., Perrin, A., and Duggan, M. (2016). Social media update 2016. Pew Research Center, November. Available at: http://www.pewinternet.org/2016/11/11/social-media-update-2016/. 7, 8

Grevet, C., Terveen, L. G., and Gilbert, E. (2014). Managing political differences in social media. In *CSCW'14: Proceedings of the 17th ACM Conference on Computer Supported Cooperative Work and Social Computing*. New York: ACM, 1400–1408. DOI: 10.1145/2531602.2531676.

Grönlund, Å. and Horan, T. A. (2005). Introducing e-Gov: History, definitions, and issues, *Communications of the Association for Information Systems*, 15(39). Available at: http://aisel.aisnet.org/cais/vol15/iss1/39. 15

Grönlund, Å. (2004). State of the art in e-Gov research – a survey. In Tranmüller, R. (Ed.), *Electronic Government: Third International Conference, EGOV 2004*, Berlin: Springer. DOI: 10.1007/978-3-540-30078-6_30. 15

Gruhl, D., Liben-Nowell, D., Guha, R. V., and Tomkins, A. (2004). Information diffusion through blogspace. *WWW'04: Proceedings of the 13th International World Wide Web Conference*. New York: ACM Press, 491–501. DOI: 10.1145/988672.988739. 44

Grunig, J. E. and Grunig, L. A. (2008). Excellence theory in public relations: Past, pPresent, and future. In A. Zerfass, B. V. Ruler, and K. Sriramesh (Eds.), *Public Relations Research*, 327–347. VS Verlag fur Sozialwissenschaften. DOI: 10.1002/9781405186407.wbiece047. 19

Gueorguieva, V. (2008). Voters, MySpace, and YouTube. *Social Science Computer Review*, 26(3), 288–300. DOI: 10.1177/0894439307305636. 53

Habermas, J. (1989). *The Structural Transformation of the Public Sphere*. Boston: MIT Press. 2, 27

Habermas, J. (2004). *The Divided West*. Malden, MA: Polity Press. 29

Hampton, K. N. and Wellman, B. (2003). Neighboring in Netville: How the Internet supports community and social capital in a wired suburb. *City and Community*, 2(4), 277–311. DOI: 10.1046/j.1535-6841.2003.00057.x. 5

Hampton, K. N., Goulet, L. S., Raine, L., and Purcell, K. (2011). Social networking sites and our lives. Pew Internet and American Life Project, June 16, 2011. http://pewinternet.org/Reports/2011/Technology-and-social-networks.aspx. 5

Hardt, M. and Negri, A. (2000). *Empire*. Harvard University Press. 35

Haridakis, P. and Hanson, G. (2009). Social interaction and co-viewing with YouTube: Blending mass communication receptions and social connection. *Journal of Broadcasting and Electronic Media*, 53(2), 317–335. DOI: 10.1080/08838150902908270. 40

Hart, W., Albarracín, D., Eagly, A. H., Brechan, I., Lindberg, M. J., and Merrill, L. (2009). Feeling validated versus being correct: A meta-analysis of selective exposure to information. *Psychological Bulletin*, 135(4), 555. DOI: 10.1037/a0015701. 70

Hemphill, L., Culotta, A., and Heston, M. (2013a). Framing in social media: How the US congress uses Twitter hashtags to frame political issues (August 28, 2013). Available at SSRN: https://ssrn.com/abstract=2317335. DOI: 10.2139/ssrn.2317335. 54

Hemphill, L., Otterbacher, J., and Shapiro, M. A. (2013b). What's Congress doing on Twitter? *CSCW'13: Proceedings of the 18th Conference on Computer Supported Cooperative Work and Social Computing*, New York: ACM Press, 877–886. DOI: 10.1145/2441776.2441876. 48

Hemphill, L. and Roback, A. J. (2014). Tweet acts: how constituents lobby congress via Twitter. *CSCW'14: Proceedings of the 17th ACM Conference on Computer Supported Cooperative Work and Social Computing*, New York: ACM Press, 1200–1210. DOI: 10.1145/2531602.2531735. 58, 59

Hemsley, J., Tanupabrungsun, S., and Semaan, B. (2017). *Proceedings of SMSociety'17: Social Media and Society*, New York: ACM, 1-10. 53

Hendricks, J. A. and Denton, R. E. (2010). Political campaigns and communicating with the electorate in the twenty-first century. In J.A. Hendricks and R.E. Denton (Eds.), *Communicator-in-Chief: How Barack Obama Used New Media Technology to Win the Whitehouse*. New York: Lexington Books. 48, 49, 51, 52

Hermans, H. J. M., and Kempen, H. J. G. (1993). *The Dialogical Self: Meaning as Movement*. San Diego: Academic Press. 38

Hillygus, D. S. and Shields, T. G. (2008). *The Persuadable Voter: Wedge Issues in Presidential Campaigns*. Princeton, NJ:Princeton University Press. DOI: 10.1515/9781400831593. 54

Himelboim, I., McCreery, S., and Smith, M. A. (2013). Birds of a feather tweet together: Integrating network and content analyses to examine cross-ideology exposure on Twitter. *Journal of Computer-Mediated Communication*, 18(2), 40–60. DOI: 10.1111/jcc4.12001. 48, 54

Hoffman, B., Robinson, H., Han, K., and Carroll, J. M. (2012). CiVicinity events: Pairing geolocation tools with a community calendar. *COM.Geo'12: Proceedings of the 3rd International Conference on Computing for Geospatial Research and Applications*, New York: ACM, Article 14, 8 pages. DOI: 10.1145/2345316.2345334. 23

Hogan, B. (2010). The presentation of self in the age of social media: Distinguishing performances and exhibitions online. *Bulletin of Science Technology and Society*, 30(6). DOI: 10.1177/0270467610385893. 37

Holt, K., Shehata, A., Strömbäck, J., and Ljungberg, E. (2013). Age and the effects of news media attention and social media use on political interest and participation: Do social media function as leveller? *European Journal of Communication*, 28(1), 19–34. DOI: 10.1177/0267323112465369. 50

Holt, R. (2004). *Dialogue on the Internet: Language, Civic Identity, and Computer–mediated Communication*. Westport, CT: Praeger. 71

Horrigan, J., Garrett, K., and Resnick, P. (2004). "The Internet and Democratic Debate," Pew Internet and American Life Project, October 27, 2004. 70

Houston, J. B., Hawthorne, J., Spialek, M. L., Greenwood, M., and McKinney, M. S. (2013). Tweeting during presidential debates: Effect on candidate evaluations and debate attitudes. *Argumentation and Advocacy*, 49, 301–311. DOI: 10.1080/00028533.2013.11821804. 62

Howard, P. N. and Hussain, M. M. (2011). The upheavals in Egypt and Tunisia: The role of digital media. *Journal of Democracy*, 22(3), 35–48. DOI: 10.1353/jod.2011.0041. 7

Hu, Y., Farnham, S. D., Monroy-Hernández, A. (2013). Whoo.ly: Facilitating information seeking for hyperlocal communities using social media. *Proceedings of CHI'13: ACM Conference on Human Factors in Computing Systems*. New York: ACM Press, 3481–3490. DOI: 10.1145/2470654.2466478. 23

Ishida, T. (2002). Digital city Kyoto. *Communications of the ACM*, 45(7), 76–81. DOI: 10.1145/514236.514238. 15

Ishida, T. and Isbister, K. (Eds) (2000). *Digital Cities: Technologies, Experiences and Future Perspectives*. Berlin: Springer. 15

Ivester, D. M. (1977). The constitutional right to know, *Hastings Constitutional Law Quarterly*, 4, 109–163. 18

Iyengar, S. and Hahn, K. S. (2009). Red media, blue media: Evidence of ideological selectivity in media use. *Journal of Communication*, 59(1), 19–39. DOI: 10.1111/j.1460-2466.2008.01402.x. 60, 72

Jaeger, P. T., Bertot, J. C., and Shuler, J. A. (2010). The Federal Depository Library Program (FDLP), Academic Libraries, and Access to Government Information. *The Journal of Academic Librarianship*, 36(6), 469–478. DOI: 10.1016/j.acalib.2010.08.002. 18

James, W. (1890). *The Principles of Psychology*. New York: Henry Holt and Company. 38

Jansen, H. J. and Koop. R. (2005). Pundits, ideologues, and ranters: The British Columbia election online. *Canadian Journal of Communication*, 30(4), 613–632. 60

Johnson, T. J. and Perlmutter, D. (2010). The Facebook election. *Mass Communication and Society*, 13, 554–559. DOI: 10.1080/15205436.2010.517490. 51, 53

Joinson, A. M. (2008). Looking at, looking up or keeping up with people?: Motives and use of Facebook. *CHI'08: Proceedings of the ACM Conference on Human-Computer Interaction*, New York: ACM, 1027–1036. DOI: 10.1145/1357054.1357213. 38

Jungherr, A. (2014). The logic of political coverage on Twitter: Temporal dynamics and content. *Journal of Communication*, 64(2), 239–259. DOI: 10.1111/jcom.12087. 54

Jürgens, P., Jungherr, A., and Schoen, H. (2011). Small worlds with a difference: new gatekeepers and the filtering of political information on Twitter. *Proceedings of the 3rd International Web Science Conference* (WebSci '11). ACM, New York, Article 21, 5 pages. DOI= 10.1145/2527031.2527034. 76

Kaid, L. L. (2006). Political web wars: The use of the internet for political advertising. In A.P. Williams and J.C. Tedesco (Eds.), *The internet Election: Perspectives on the Web in Campaign 2004*, (pp. 67–82). Lanham, MD: Rowman and Littlefield. 52

Kamarck, E. C. (1999). Campaigning on the Internet in the elections of 1998. In E.C. Kamarck and J. J. S. Nye (Eds.), *Democracy.Com?: Governance in the Network World*, 99–123. Hollis, NH: Hollis Publishing. 51

Karkın, N., Yavuz, N., Parlak, İ, and İkiz, Ö.Ö. (2015). Twitter use by politicians during social uprisings: an analysis of Gezi park protests in Turkey. *Proceedings of the 16th Annual International Conference on Digital Government Research* (dg.o '15). New York: ACM, 20–28. DOI: 10.1145/2757401.2757430. 7, 64

Katz, E. (1959). Mass communication research and the study of culture. *Studies in Public Communication*, 2, 1–6. 38, 39

Katz, E., Blumler, J. and Gurevitch, M. (1973). Uses and gratifications research. *The Public Opinion Quarterly*, 37(4), 509–523. DOI: 10.1086/268109. 38, 39

Kaufhold, K., Valenzuela, S., and Gil de Zúñiga, H. (2010). Effects of citizen and professional journalism on political knowledge and participation. *Journalism and Mass Communication Quarterly* 87(3), 515–529. DOI: 10.1177/107769901008700305. 3

Kavanaugh, A., Ahuja, A., Gad, S., Neidig, S., Pérez-Quiñones, M. A., Ramakrishnan, N., and Tedesco, J. (2014). (Hyper) local news aggregation: Designing for social affordances. *Government Information Quarterly*, 31(1), 30–41. DOI: 10.1016/j.giq.2013.04.004. 23

Kavanaugh, A., Carroll, J. M., Rosson, M. B., and Zin, T. T. (2006). Community networks: Where offline communities meet offline. *Journal of Computer-Mediated Communication*, 10(4). DOI: 10.1111/j.1083-6101.2005.tb00266.x.

Kavanaugh, A. and Patterson, S. J. (2001). The impact of community computer networks on social capital and community involvement. *American Behavioral Scientist*, 45(3), 496–509. DOI: 10.1177/00027640121957312. 18

Kavanaugh, A., Sheetz, S. D., Skandrani, H., Tedesco, J. C., Sun, Y., and Fox, E. A. (2016). The use and impact of social media during the 2011 Tunisian Revolution. *Proceedings of the*

17th International Digital Government Research Conference on Digital Government Research (dg.o '16), Yushim Kim and Monica Liu (Eds.), ACM, New York, 20–30. DOI: 10.1145/2912160.2912175. 7, 65

Kavanaugh, A. L., Reese, D. D., Carroll, J. M., and Rosson, M. B. (2005). Weak ties in networked communities. *The Information Society*, 21(2), 119-131. DOI: 10.1080/01972240590925320. 5

Kaye, B. and Johnson, T. (2002). Online and in the know: Uses and gratifications of the Web for political information. *Journal of Broadcasting and Electronic Media*, 46(1), 54–71. DOI: 10.1207/s15506878jobem4601_4. 55

Keeter, S., Zukin, C., Andolina, M., and Jenkins, K. (2002). The civic and political health of the nation: A generational portrait. Center for Information and Research on Civic Learning and Engagement. Available at: http://civicyouth.org/research/products/Civic_Political_Health.pdf.

Kelly, J., Fisher, D., and Smith, M. (2005). Debate, division, and diversity: Political discourse networks in USENET newsgroups. *Stanford Online Deliberation Conference DIAC'05*. 70

Kenski, K. and Conway, B. A. (2016). Social media and elections. In *Praeger Handbook of Political Campaigning in the United States*, ABC-CLIO, 191–208. 53

Kenski, K. and Stroud, N. J. (2010). Connections between internet use and political efficacy, knowledge, and participation. *Journal of Broadcasting and Electronic Media*, 50, 173–192. DOI: 10.1207/s15506878jobem5002_1. 5

Khamis, S. and Vaughn, K. (2011). Cyberactivism in the Egyptian revolution: How civic engagement and citizen journalism tilted the balance. *Arab Media & Society*, 14(3), 1–25. 7

Kim, D. H. and Pasek, J. (2016). Explaining the diversity deficit: Value-trait consistency in news exposure and democratic citizenship. *Communication Research*, DOI: 10.1177/0093650216644647. 72

Kim, H. and Bearman, P. S. (1997). The structure and dynamics of movement participation. *American Sociological Review*, 62(1), 70–93. DOI: 10.2307/2657453. 54

King, S. F. and Brown, P. (2007). Fix my street or else: Using the internet to voice public service concerns. *Proceedings of ICEGOV'07: 1st International Conference on Theory and Practice of Electronic Governance*. New York: ACM Press, 72-80. DOI: 10.1145/1328057.1328076. 20

Kiousis, S. (2004). Explicating media salience: A factor analysis of New York Times issue coverage during the 2000 U.S. presidential election. *Journal of Communication*, 54(1), 71–87. DOI: 10.1111/j.1460-2466.2004.tb02614.x. 41

Kiousis, S. and McCombs, M. (2004). Agenda-setting effects and attitude strength.: Political figures during the 1996 presidential election. *Communication Research*, 31(1), 36–57. DOI: 10.1177/0093650203260205. 41

Kitchens, J. T., Powell, L., and Williams, G. (2003). Information please? Information seeking, mass media, and he undecided voter. *Communication Research Reports*, 20, 73-81. DOI: 10.1080/08824090309388801. 56

Klinenberg, E. and Perrin, A. (2000). Symbolic politics in the information age: The 1996 Republican presidential campaigns in cyberspace. *Information, Communication and Society*, 3(1), 17–38. DOI: 10.1080/136911800359400. 51

Klofstad, C. A. (2011). *Civic Talk: Peers, Politics, and the Future of Democracy*. Philadelphia, PA: Temple University Press. 50

Kluver, R., Jankowski, N., Foot, K., and Schneider, S. M. (Eds.) (2007). *The Internet and National Elections. A Comparative Study of Web Campaigning*. Routledge. 48

Knobloch-Westerwick, S. and Meng, J. (2009). Looking the other way: Selective exposure to attitude-consistent and couterattitudinal political information. *Communication Research*, 36(3). DOI: 10.1177/0093650209333030. 70

Kobayashi, T. and Ikeda, K. (2009). Selective exposure in political web browsing. *Information, Communication and Society*, 12(6), 929–953. DOI: 10.1080/13691180802158490. 70

Kohut, A. (1999). *The Internet News Audience Goes Odinary*. Washington, D.C.: The Pew Research Center. 18

Korn, M. and Voida, A. (2015). Creating friction: Infrastructuring civic engagement in everyday life. *Proceedings of AA'15: The Fifth Decennial Aarhus Conference on Critical Alternatives*, 145–156. DOI: 10.7146/aahcc.v1i1.21198. 4

Kossinets, G. and Watts, D. (2009). Origins of homophily in an evolving social network. *American Journal of Sociology*, 115(2), 405–450. DOI: 10.1086/599247. 44, 69

Kow, Y. M., Kou, Y., Semaan, B., and Cheng, W. (2016). Mediating the undercurrents: Using social media to sustain a social movement. *CHI'16: Proceedings of the ACM Conference on Human Factors in Computing Systems*. New York: ACM, 3883–3894. DOI: 10.1145/2858036.2858186. 66

Kraemer, K. and King, J. L. (2006). Information technology and administrative reform: Will e-government be different? *International Journal of Electronic Government Research*, 2(1), 20 pages. DOI: 10.4018/jegr.2006010101. 16

Kreiss, D. (2014). Seizing the moment: The presidential campaigns' use of Twitter during the 2012 electoral cycle. *New Media and Society*, 18(8), 1473–1490. DOI: 10.1177/1461444814562445. 53

Kriplean, T., Morgan, J., Freelon, D., Borning, A., and Bennett, L. (2012). Supporting reflective public thought with ConsiderIt. *CSCW'12: Proceedings of the ACM Conference on Computer Supported Cooperative Work*. New York: ACM. 265-274. DOI: 10.1145/2145204.2145249. 71

Krueger, B. S. (2002). Assessing the potential of Internet political participation in the United States: A resource approach. *American Politics Research*, 30, 476–498. DOI: 10.1177/1532673X02030005002. 3

LaCour, M. (2012). A balanced news diet, not selective exposure: Evidence from a direct measure of media exposure. *APSA 2012 Annual Meeting Paper*, 15(5), 795–825. DOI: 10.2139/ssrn.2050762. 60

LaRose, R. and Eastin, M. S. (2004). A social cognitive theory of internet uses and gratifications: Toward a new model of media attendance. *Journal of Broadcasting and Electronic Media*, 48 (3), 358–377. DOI: 10.1207/s15506878jobem4803_2. 39

Latour, B. (2005). *Reassembling the Social: An Introduction to Actor-Network Theory*. Oxford University Press. 43

Lee, N-J. and Oh, S. T. (2012). To personalize or depersonalize: When and how politicians personalized tweets affect the public's reactions. *Journal of Communication*, 62, 932–949. DOI: 10.1111/j.1460-2466.2012.01681.x. 58

Lee, N-J., Shah, D. V., and McLeod, J. M. (2013). Processes of political socialization: A communication mediation approach to youth civic engagement. *Communication Research*, 40(5), 669–697. DOI: 10.1177/0093650212436712. 39

Leskovec, J., Adamic, L., and Huberman B. (2007a). The dynamics of viral marketing. *ACM Transactions on the Web*, 1(1). DOI: 10.1145/1232722.1232727. 44

Leskovec, J., McGlohon, M., Faloutsos, C., Glance, N., and Hurst, M. (2007b). Cascading behavior in large blog graphs. *Proceedings of SIAM International Conference on Data Mining*. DOI: 10.1137/1.9781611972771.60. 44

Leskovec, J., Backstrom, L. and Kleinberg, J. (2009). Meme-tracking and the dynamics of the news cycle. *SIGKDD'09: Proceedings of the 15th ACM International Conference on Knowledge Discovery and Data Mining*. DOI: 10.1145/1557019.1557077. 44

Liao, Q. V. and Fu, W-T. (2014). Can you hear me now? Mitigating the echo chamber effect by source position indicators. *CSCW 2014: Proceedings of the 17th ACM Conference on Com-*

puter Supported Cooperative Work and Social Computing. New York: ACM Press. 184–196. DOI: 10.1145/2531602.2531711. 71

Lim, M. (2012). Clicks, cabs, and coffee houses: Social media and oppositional movements in Egypt, 2004-2011. *Journal of Communication*, 62(2), 231–248. DOI: 10.1111/j.1460-2466.2012.01628.x. 7

Lim, J. (2006). A Cross lagged analysis of agenda setting among online media. *Journalism and Mass Communication Quarterly*, 83(2), 298–312. DOI: 10.1177/107769900608300205. 41

Lin, N. (2001). *Social Capital: A Theory of Social Structure and Action.* Cambridge: Cambridge University Press. DOI: 10.1017/CBO9780511815447. 36

Lin, N. (2008). A network theory of social capital. In D. Castiglione, J. W. van Deth and G. Wolleb (Eds.), *The Handbook of Social Capital* (pp. 50–69). London: Oxford University Press. 36

Linders, D. (2012). From e-government to we-government: Defining a typology for citizen coproduction in the age of social media. *Government Information Quarterly*, 29(4), 446–454. DOI: 10.1016/j.giq.2012.06.003. 19

Linturi, R., Koivunen, M-R., and Sulkanen, J. (1999). Helsinki arena 2000 – Augmenting a real city to a virtual one. In T. Ishida and K. Isbister (Eds.), Digital cities: Technologies, experiences, and future perspectives. (pp 83–96), *Lecture Notes in Computer Science*, vol. 1765. DOI: 10.1007/3-540-46422-0_8. 15

Lippmann, W. (1925). *The Phantom Public.* Transaction Publishing. 58

Litt, E. (2012). Knock, knock. Who's there? The imagined audience. *Journal of Broadcasting and Electronic Media*, 56, 330–345. DOI: 10.1080/08838151.2012.705195. 37

Litt, E. and Harrgitai, E. (2016). The imagined audience on social network sites. *Social Media and Society*, 2 (1). DOI: 10.1177/2056305116633482. 38

Lloyd, L., Kaulgud, P., and Skiena, S. (2006, March). Newspapers vs. blogs: Who gets the scoop? Paper presented at the *AAAI Symposium in Computational Approaches to Analysing Weblogs*, Stanford, CA. 42

Lupia, A. (2001). *Evaluation: The Web White and Blue Network 2000.* Available at: https://www.markle.org/sites/default/files/wwbevaluation.pdf. 48

Lyotard, J. F. (1984). *The Postmodern Condition.* Minneapolis, MN: University of Minnesota Press. 32

Macek, J. (2013). More than a desire for text: Online participation and the social curation of content. *Convergence*, 19, 295–302. DOI: 10.1177/1354856513486530. 43

Macek, J. (2015). Social media and diffused participation. In P. Lorentz, D. Šmahel, M. Metyková, and M. Wright (eds), *Living in the Digital Age: Self-presentation, Networking, Playing, and Participating in Politics* (pp. 196–209). Brno: MUNI Press. 42

Madison, D. S. and Hamera, J. (Eds.). (2006). *The SAGE Handbook of Performance Studies.* Thousand Oaks, CA: SAGE Publicatons. 37

Maeda, H., Sekimoto, Y., and Seto, T. (2016). Lightweight road manager: Smartphone-based automatic determination of road damage status by deep neural network. *MobiGIS'16: Proceedings of the 5th ACM SIGSPATIAL International Workshop on Mobile Geographic Information Systems.* New York: ACM, 37–45. DOI: 10.1145/3004725.3004729. 20

Mahoney, J., Feltwell, T., Ajuruchi, O., and Lawson, S. (2016). Constructing the visual online political self: An analysis of Instagram use by the Scottish electorate. *CHI'16: Proceedings of the 2016 ACM Conference on Human Factors in Computing Systems.* New York: ACM, 3339–3351. DOI: 10.1145/2858036.2858160. 79

Marchi, R. (2012). With Facebook, blogs, and fake news, teens reject journalistic "objectivity." *Journal of Communication* Inquiry, 36(3), 246–262. DOI: 10.1177/0196859912458700. 77

Margolis, M. and Resnick, D. (2000). *Politics as Usual: The Cyberspace "Revolution."* Sage Publications. 52

Margolis, M., Resnick, D., and Wolfe, J.D. (1999). Party competition on the Internet in the United States and Britain. *Harvard International Journal of Press-Politics*, 4(4), 24–47. DOI: 10.1177/1081180X9900400403.

Maruyama, M., Robertson, Scott P., Douglas, S., Raine, R., and Semaan, B. (2017). Social watching a civic broadcast: Understanding the effects of positive feedback and other users' opinions. *CSCW'17: Proceedings of the ACM Conference on Computer Supported Cooperative Work and Social Media*, New York: ACM, 794–807. DOI: 10.1145/2998181.2998340. 61, 62

Marwick, A. E. and boyd, d. (2011). I tweet honestly, I tweet passionately: Twitter users, context collapse, and the imagined audience. *New Media and Society*, 13(1), 114–133. DOI: 10.1177/1461444810365313. 37, 53

Marwick, A. E. and boyd, d. (2014). Networked privacy: How teenagers negotiate context in social media. *New Media and Society*, 16(7), 1051–1067. DOI: 10.1177/1461444814543995. 38

Mascaro, C., Agosto, D., and Goggins, S. P. (2016). One-Sided Conversations: The 2012 Presidential Election on Twitter. *Proceedings of the 17th International Digital Government Research Conference on Digital Government Research* (dg.o '16), Yushim Kim and Monica Liu (Eds.), ACM, New York, 112–121. DOI: 10.1145/2912160.2912185. 58

Masden, C. A., Grevet, C., Grinter, R. E., Gilbert, E. and Edwards, W. K. (2014). Tensions in scaling-up community social media: A multi-neighborhood study of Nextdoor. *Proceedings of CHI'14: The ACM Conference on Human Factors in Computing Systems*, 3239–3248. DOI: 10.1145/2556288.2557319. 23

McCombs, M. (2014). *Setting the Agenda*. Polity Press.

McCombs, M. and Shaw, D. (1972). The agenda-setting role of mass media. *Public Opinion Quarterly*, 36(1), 76–187. 41

McCombs, M. E. and D. L. Shaw. (1993). The evolution of agenda-setting research: Twenty-five years in the marketplace of ideas. *Journal of Communication*, 43(2), 58–67. DOI: 10.1111/j.1460-2466.1993.tb01262.x. 41

McDermott, P. (2010). Building open government. *Government Information Quarterly* 27(4), 401–413 . DOI: 10.1016/j.giq.2010.07.002. 18

McKinney, M. S. and Chattopadhyay, S. (2007). Political engagement through debates: Young citizens' reactions to the 2004 presidential debates. *American Behavioral Scientist*, 50, 1169–118. DOI: 10.1177/0002764207300050. 62

McLaughlin, L. (2004). Feminism and the political economy of transnational public space. *The Sociological Review*, 52(1), 156–175. DOI: 10.1111/j.1467-954X.2004.00478.x. 29

McLeod, J. M., Scheufele, D., and Moy, P. (1999). Community, communication and participation: The role of mass media and interpersonal discussion in local political participation. *Political Communication*, 16, 315–336. DOI: 10.1080/105846099198659. 50

McPherson, M., Smith-Lovin, L., and Brashears, M. E. (2006). Social isolation in America: Changes in core discussion networks over two decades. *American Sociological Review*, 71(3), 353–375. DOI: 10.1177/000312240607100301. 49

McPherson, M., Smith-Lovin, L., and Cook, J. M. (2001). Birds of a feather: Homophily in social networks. *Annual Review of Sociology*, 27, 415–444. DOI: 10.1146/annurev.soc.27.1.415. 69

Meijer, A. J., Curtin, D., and Hillebrandt, M. 2012. Open government: connecting vision and voice. *International Review of Administrative Sciences*, 78(1), 10–29. DOI: 10.1177/0020852311429533. 18

Meijer, A. J. and Thaens, M. (2013). Social media strategies: Understanding the differences between North American police departments. *Government Information Quarterly*, 30(4), 343–350. DOI: 10.1016/j.giq.2013.05.023. 8

Meraz, S. (2009). Is there an elite hold? Traditional media to social media agenda setting influence in blog networks. *Journal of Computer-Mediated Communication*, 14(3), 682–707. DOI: 10.1111/j.1083-6101.2009.01458.x. 41

Meraz, S. (2011). The fight for "how to think": Traditional media, social networks, and issue interpretation. *Journalism*, 12(1), 107–127. DOI: 10.1177/1464884910385193. 42

Meraz, S. and Papacharissi, Z. (2013). Networked gatekeeping and networked framing on #Egypt. *The International Journal of Press/Politics*, 18(2), 138–166. DOI: 10.1177/1940161212474472. 42

Mergel, I. (2013a). A framework for interpreting social media interactions in the public sector. *Government Information Quarterly*, 30(4), 327–334. DOI: 10.1016/j.giq.2013.05.015. 8, 19

Mergel, I. (2013b). Social media adoption and resulting tactics in the US federal government. *Government Information Quarterly*, 30(2), 123–130. DOI: 10.1016/j.giq.2012.12.004. 8

Messing, S. and Westwood, S. J. (2014). Selective exposure in the age of social media: Endorsements trump partisan source affiliation when selecting news online. *Communication Research*, 41(8), 1042–1063. DOI: 10.1177/0093650212466406. 50, 60, 72

Metaxas, P. T. and Mustafaraj, E. (2010). From obscurity to prominence in minutes: Political speech and real-time search. *Proceedings WebSci10: Extending the Frontiers of Society*, Available at http:// bit.ly/ 2n1IEUC. 76

Mihailidis, P. (2014). A tethered generation: Exploring the role of mobile phones in the daily life of young people. *Mobile Media and Communication*, 2(1), 58–72. DOI: 10.1177/2050157913505558. 40

Mondal, M., Silva, L. A., and Benevenuto, F. (2017). A measurement study of hate speech in social media. *Proceedings of HT'17: The 28th ACM Conference on Hypertext and Social Media*. New York: ACM Press, 85–94. DOI: 10.1145/3078714.3078723. 79

Monroy-Hernández, A., boyd, d., Kiciman, E., De Choudhury, M., and Counts, S. (2013). The new war correspondents: the rise of civic media curation in urban warfare. *Proceedings of CSCW'13: The ACM Conference on Computer Supported Cooperative Work*. New York: ACM Press, 1443–1452. DOI: 10.1145/2441776.2441938. 67

Morozov, E. (2009). The brave new world of slacktivism. *Foreign Policy*. (May 19). Available at: http://foreignpolicy.com/2009/05/19/the-brave-new-world-of-slacktivism/. 8

Morris, D. S. and Morris, J. S. (2013). Digital inequality and participation in the political process. Real or imagined? *Social Science Computer Review*, 31(5), 589–600. DOI: 10.1177/0894439313489259. 50

Mossberger, K., Wu, Y., and Crawford, J. (2013). Connecting citizens and local governments? Social media and interactivity in major U.S. cities. *Government Information Quarterly*, 34(4), 351–358. DOI: 10.1016/j.giq.2013.05.016. 8

Mouffe, C. (2000). Deliberative democracy or agonistic pluralism. *HIS Political Science Series*. (December). Available at: http://irihs.ihs.ac.at/1312/1/pw_72.pdf. 32

Mouffe, C. (2005). *On the Political: Thinking in Action*. London: Routledge. 32

Munson, S. A., Lee, S. Y., and Resnick, P. (2013). Encouraging reading of diverse political viewpoints with a browser widget. *Proceedings of ICWSM 2013: The 7th International Conference on Weblogs and Social Media*. AAAI Press, 419–428. 69

Munson, S. A. and Resnick, P. (2010). Presenting diverse political opinions: How and how much. *Proceedings of CHI '10: The ACM Conference on Human Factors in Computing Systems*. New York: ACM, 1457–1466. DOI: 10.1145/1753326.1753543. 70, 71

Mustafaraj, E. and Metaxas, P. T. (2017). The fake news spreading plague: Was it preventable? *Proceedings of WebSci'17: The ACM Conference on Web Science*. New York: ACM Press. 235–239. DOI: 10.1145/3091478.3091523. 76

Mutz, D. C. and Martin, P. S. (2001). Facilitating communication across lines of political difference: The role of mass media. *American Political Science Review*, 95(1), 97–114. 70

Mutz, D. C. and Young, L. (2011). Communication and public opinion: Plus Ça Change? *Public Opinion Quarterly*, 75(5), 1018–1044. DOI: 10.1093/poq/nfr052. 77

Nahon, K. and Hemsley, J. (2013). *Going Viral*. Wiley. 76

Naphade, M., Banavar, G., Harrison, C., Paraszczak, J. and Morris, R. (2011). Smarter cities and their innovation challenges. *Computer*, 44(6), 32–39. DOI: 10.1109/MC.2011.187. 20

Narwal, V., Salih, M. H., Lopez, J. A., Ortega, A., O'Donovan, J., Höllerer, T., and Savage, S. (2017). Automated assistants to identify and prompt action on visual news bias. *Proceedings of CHI'17: ACM Conference on Human Factors in Computing Systems*. New York: ACM Press, 2796–2801. DOI: 10.1145/3027063.3053227. 79

Nekrasov, M., Parks, L., and Belding, E. (2017). Limits to internet freedoms: Being heard in an increasingly authoritarian world. *Proceedings of LIMITS'17: Workshop on Computing Within Limits*, New York: ACM Press. 119–128. DOI: 10.1145/3080556.3080564. 79

Newman, N. (2017). Reuters Institute Digital News Report 2017. Reuters Institute for the Study of Journalism. Available at: https://reutersinstitute.politics.ox.ac.uk/sites/default/files/Digital%20News%20Report%202017%20web_0.pdf. 75, 76

Neuman, R. W., Guggenheim, L., Mo Jang, S., and Young Bae, S. (2014). The dynamics of public attention: Agenda-setting theory meets big data. *Journal of Communication*, 64(2), 194–214. DOI: 10.1111/jcom.12088. 41

Nisbet, E. C., Stoycheff, E. and Pearce, K. E. (2012). Internet use and democratic demands: A multinational, multilevel model of internet use and citizen attitudes about democracy. *Journal of Communication*, 62 (2), 249–265. DOI: 10.1111/j.1460-2466.2012.01627.x. 3

Norris, P. (2000). *A Virtuous Circle: Political Communications in Postindustrial Societies*. Cambridge: Cambridge University Press. DOI: 10.1017/CBO9780511609343. 3, 48

Norris, P. (2001). *Digital Divide: Civic Engagement, Information Poverty, and Internet Worldwide*. New York: Cambridge University Press. DOI: 10.1017/CBO9781139164887. 3, 4, 49, 73

Norris, P. (2003). Preaching to the converted? Pluralism, participation and party websites. *Party Politics*, 9(1), 21–45. DOI: 10.1177/135406880391003. 48

Nothhaft, H. (2016). The dream of enlightenment within digital reach? Concepts of modern democracy. In W.T. Coombs, J. Falkheimer, M. Heide, and P. Young, (Eds.), *Strategic Communication, Social Media and Democracy: The Challenge of the Digital Naturals*. New York: Routledge. 35

Noveck, B. S. (2000). Paradoxical partners: Electronic communication and electronic democracy. *Democratization*, 7(1), 18–35. DOI: 10.1080/13510340008403643. 70

Oldenburg, R. (1999). *The Great Good Place: Cafes, Coffee Shops, Bookstores, Bars, Hair Salons and Other Hangouts at the Heart of a Community* (2nd ed.). New York: Marlowe and Company. 32

Olteanu, A., Talamadupula, K., and Varshney, K. R. (2017). The limits of abstract evaluation metrics: The case of hate speech detection. *Proceedings of WebSci'17: ACM Conference on Web Science*, New York: ACM Press, 405–406. DOI: 10.1145/3091478.3098871. 79

Olteanu, A., Vieweg, S., and Castillo, C. (2015). What to Expect When the Unexpected Happens: Social Media Communications Across Crises. *Proceedings of CSCW'15: The 18th ACM Conference on Computer Supported Cooperative Work and Social Computing*, New York: ACM Press, 994–1009. DOI: 10.1145/2675133.2675242. 66

Östman, J. (2012). Information, expression, participation: How involvement in user-generated content relates to democratic engagement among young people. *New Media and Society*, 14, 1004–1021. DOI: 10.1177/1461444812438212. 40

Pancer, S. M., Pratt, M., Hunsberger, B., and Alisat, S. (2007). Community and political involvement in adolescence: What distinguishes the activists from the uninvolved? *Journal of Community Psychology*, 35(6), 741–759. DOI: 10.1002/jcop.20176. 50

Papacharissi, Z. (2002). The virtual sphere: The internet as a public sphere. *New Media Society*, 4(1), 9–27. doi: DOI: 10.1177/14614440222226244. 2, 49

Papacharissi, Z. (2004). Democracy online: Civility, politeness, and the democratic potential of online political discussion groups. *New Media and Society*, 6(2), 259–283. DOI: 10.1177/1461444804041444. 32

Papacharissi, Z. (2009). The virtual sphere 2.0. The Internet, the public sphere, and beyond. In A. Chadwick and P. N. Howard (Eds.), *Routledge Handbook of Internet Politics*, (pp. 230–245). New York:Routledge. 2, 31, 32Papacharissi, Z. (2010). *A Private Sphere: Democracy in a Digital Age*. Polity Press. 2, 3

Papacharissi, Z. (2012). Without you, I'm nothing: Performances of the self on Twitter. *International Journal of Communication*, 6, 1989–2006. 31, 37

Papacharissi, Z. (2013). A networked self: identity performance and sociability on social network sites. In F. L.F. Lee, L. Leung, J. L. Qiu, D. S.C. Chu (Eds.), *Frontiers in New Media Research*. (pp. 207–221). New York: Routledge.

Papacharissi, Z. and Easton, E. (2012). In the habitus of the new: Agency, structure, and the social media habitus. In J. Hartley, A. Bruns, and J. Burgess (Eds.), *New Media Dynamics*. Malden, MA: Blackwell. 37

Papacharissi, Z. and Mendelson, A. (2011). Toward a new(er) sociability: Uses, gratifications and social capital on Facebook. In S. Papathanassopoulos (Ed.), *Media Perspectives for the 21st Century*, New York: Routledge. 39

Papacharissi, Z. and Rubin, A. M. (2000), Predictors of internet use, *Journal of Broadcasting and Electronic Media*, 44(2),175–196. DOI: 10.1207/s15506878jobem4402_2. 39, 40

Pariser, E. (2011). *The Filter Bubble: What the Internet is Hiding from You*. London: Penguin UK. 54

Park, C. P. (2013). Does Twitter motivate involvement in politics? Tweeting, opinion leadership, and political engagement. *Computers in Human Behavior*, 29, 1641–1648. DOI: 10.1016/j.chb.2013.01.044. 60

Park, S., Kang, S., Chung, S., Song, J. (2009). NewsCube: Delivering multiple aspects of news to mitigate media bias. *Proceedings of CHI'09: The 27th International Conference on Human Factors in Computing Systems*. New York: ACM Press, 443–452. DOI: 10.1145/1518701.1518772.

Park, N., Kee, K., and Valenzuela, S. (2009). Being immersed in social networking environment:-Facebook groups, uses and gratifications, and social outcomes. *CyberPsychology and Behavior*, 12(6), 729–733. DOI: 10.1089/cpb.2009.0003. 39, 40, 69

Parker, B. J. and Plank, R. E. (2000). A uses and gratifications perspective on the Internet as a new information source. *American Business Review*, 18(2), 43–49. 39

Parks, W. (1957). The open government principle: Applying the right to know under the constitution, *George Washington Law Review*, 26(1), 1–22. 18

Parmelee, J. H. (2013). The agenda-building function of political tweets. *New Media and Society*, 16(3), 434–450. DOI:10.1177/1461444813487955. 41, 42, 53, 55

Parmelee, J. H. (2014). The agenda-building function of political tweets. *New Media and Society*, 16(3), 434–450. DOI: 10.1177/1461444813487955.

Parmelee, J. H., and Bichard, S.L. (2013). *Politics and the Twitter Revolution: How Tweets Influence the Relationship between Political Leaders and the Public*. Lanham, MD: Lexington Books. 59

Pasek, J., Moore, E., Romer, D. (2009). Realizing the social Internet? Online social networking meets offline civic engagement. *Journal of Information Technology and Politics*, 6, 197–215. DOI: 10.1080/19331680902996403. 50

Patterson, S. and Kavanaugh, A. (2001). Building critical mass in community computer networks. *Electronic Journal of Communication*. 18

Perrin, A. (2015). Social networking usage: 2005-2015. Pew Research Center. October. Available at: http://www.pewinternet.org/2015/10/08/2015/Social-Networking-Usage-2005-2015/. 7

Polat, R. K. (2005). The Internet and political participation: Exploring the explanatory links. *European Journal of Communication*, 20, 435–459. DOI: 10.1177/0267323105058251. 3

Poor, N. (2005). Mechanisms of an online public sphere: The website Slashdot. *Journal of Computer-Mediated Communication*, 10(2), DOI: 10.1111/j.1083-6101.2005.tb00241.x. 2

Poster, M. (1997). Cyberdemocracy: Internet and the public sphere, in D. Porter (Ed.), *Internet Culture* (pp. 201–18). New York: Routledge. 32

Powell, L., Richmond, V. P., and Williams, G. C. (2011). Social networking and political campaigns: Perceptions of candidates as interpersonal constructs. *North American Journal of Psychology*, 13(2), 331–342. 56

Putnam, R. D. (1995). Tuning in, tuning out: the strange disappearance of social capital in America. *PS: Political Science and Politics*, 28(4), p. 664–683. DOI: 10.1017/S1049096500058856. 3, 36

Putnam, R. D. (2000). *Bowling Alone: The Collapse and Revival of American Community*. Simon and Schuster, New York. DOI: 10.1145/358916.361990. 3, 49, 69

Qu, Y., Huang, C., Zhang, P., and Zhang, J. (2011). Microblogging after a major disaster in China: a case study of the 2010 Yushu earthquake. *Proceedings of CSCW'11: The ACM Conference on Computer Supported Cooperative Work*, New York: ACM Press, 25–34. DOI: 10.1145/1958824.1958830. 66

Quinteller, E. and Vissers, S. (2008). The effect of internet use on political participation: An analysis of survey results for 16-year-olds in Belgium. *Social Science Computer Review*, 26(4), 411–427. DOI: 10.1177/0894439307312631. 40

Raine, L. and Smith, A. (2012). Politics on social networking sites, Pew Internet and American Life Project, Sept. 4, 2012. Available at: http://pewinternet.org/Reports/2012/Politics-on-SNS.aspx. 5, 8

Resnick, P. (2001). Beyond bowling together: Sociotechnical capital, in J. Carroll (ed.), *HCI in the New Millennium*, (pp. 247–272). Boston, MA:Addison-Wesley. 5

Rheingold, H. (2000). T*he Virtual Community: Homesteading on the Electronic Frontier*. Cambridge, MA: MIT Press. 3

Rheingold, H. (2002). *Smart Mobs. The Next Social Revolution*. Cambridge, MA: Perseus. 32

Ritzer, G. and Jurgenson, N. (2010). Production, consumption, presumption: The nature of capitalism in the age of the digital "prosumer." *Journal of Consumer Culture*, 10(13), 13–36. DOI: 10.1177/1469540509354673. 6

Roback, A. and Hemphill, L. (2013). "I'd have to vote against you": Issue campaigning via Twitter. *Proceedings of CSCW'13: ACM Conference on Computer Supported Cooperative Work*, New York: ACM Press, 259–262. DOI 10.1145/2441955.2442016. 58

Roberts, M., Wanta, W. and Dzwo, T-H. (2002). Agenda setting and issue salience online. *Communication Research*, 29(1), 452–465. DOI: 10.1177/0093650202029004004. 41

Robertson, S. P., Douglas, S., Maruyama, M., and Chen, L. (2012). Political dialog evolution in a social network. *Proceedings of the 13th Annual International Conference on Digital Government Research*, New York: ACM, 40–48. DOI: 10.1145/2307729.2307737. 58

Robertson, S. P., Douglas, S., Maruyama, M., and Semaan, B. (2013). Political discourse on social networking sites: Sentiment, in-group/out-group orientation, and rationality. *Information Polity*, 18(2), 107–126. DOI: 10.3233/IP-130303. 58

Robinson, D. G., Yu, H., Zeller, W. P., Felton, E. W. (2009). Government data and the invisible hand. *Yale Journal of Law and Technology*, 11, 160–176. 18

Rogers, E. (1995). *Diffusion of Innovations*. 4th ed. Free Press. 44

Rogers, E. M., Collins-Jarvis, L. and Schmitz, J. (1994). The PEN Project in Santa Monica: Interactive communication, equality, and political action. *Journal of the American Society for Information Science*, 45(6), 401–410. DOI: 10.1002/(SICI)1097-4571(199407)45:6<401::AID-ASI6>3.0.CO;2-N. 13

Romero, D. M., Galuba, W., Asur, S., and Huberman, B. A. (2011a). Influence and passivity in social media. *Proceedings of ECML PKDD 2011: Machine Learning and Knowledge Discovery in Databases - European Conference, Lecture Notes in Computer Science*, 6913, 18–33. DOI: 10.1007/978-3-642-23808-6_2. 44

Romero, D. M., Meeder, B., and Kleinberg, J. (2011b). Differences in the mechanics of information diffusion across topics: Idioms, political hashtags, and complex contagion on Twitter, *WWW'04: Proceedings of the 20th International World Wide Web Conference*. New York: ACM Press, 695–704. DOI: 10.1145/1963405.1963503. 44

Rorissa, A., Demissie, D., and Pardo, T. A. (2011). Benchmarking e-government: A comparison of frameworks for computing e-government index and ranking. *Government Information Quarterly*, 28(3), 354–362. DOI: 10.1016/j.giq.2010.09.006. 16

Rossini, P. G. C, Hemsley, J., Tanuprabrungsun, S., Zhang, F., Robinson, J., and Stromer-Galley, J. (2017). Social media, U.S. presidential campaigns, and public opinion polls: Disentangling effects. *Proceedings of Social Media and Society*. New York: ACM, 1–5. DOI: 10.1145/3097286.3097342. 52

Rubin, A. (1993). Audience activity and media use. *Journal of Communication Monographs*, 60(1), 98–105. DOI: 10.1080/03637759309376300. 38

Rubin, A. (2002). The Uses-and-Gratifications perspective of media effects. In J. Bryant, M.B. Oliver, J. Bryant, and D. Zillmann (Eds.), *Media Effects: Advances in Theory and Research*. Taylor and Francis. 39

Ruggiero, T. (2000). Uses and gratification theory in the 21st century. *Mass Communication and Society*, 3(1), 3–37. DOI: 10.1207/S15327825MCS0301_02. 39

Saez-Trumper, D., Castillo, C., and Lalmas. M. (2013). Social media news communities: Gatekeeping, coverage, and statement bias. In CIKM. DOI: 10.1145/2505515.2505623.

Sarcevic, A., Palen, L., White, J., Starbird, K., Bagdouri, M., and Anderson, K. (2012). "Beacons of hope" in decentralized coordination: learning from on-the-ground medical twitters during the 2010 Haiti earthquake. *Proceedings of CSCW'12: The ACM Conference on Computer Supported Cooperative Work*, New York: ACM Press, 47–56. DOI: 10.1145/2145204.2145217. 66

Scheitle, C. P. (2011). Google's insights for search: A note evaluating the use of search engine data in social research. *Social Science Quarterly*, 92(1), 285–295. DOI: 10.1111/j.1540-6237.2011.00768.x. 56

Scherer, S., Wimmer, M. A. and Strykowski, S. (2015). Social government: a concept supporting communities in co-creation and co-production of public services. *Proceedings of the 16th Annual International Conference on Digital Government Research* (dg.o '15). ACM, New York, NY, USA, 204–209. DOI: 10.1145/2757401.2757417. 19

Scheufele, D. A. and Tewksbury, D. (2007). Framing, agenda setting, and priming: The evolution of three media effects models. *Journal of Communication*, 57(1), 9–20. DOI: 10.1111/j.0021-9916.2007.00326.x. 54

Scheufele, D. A., Hardy, B. W., Brossard, D., Waismel-Manor, I. S., and Nisbet, E. (2006). Democracy based on difference: Examining the links between structural heterogeneity, heterogeneity of discussion networks, and democratic citizenship. *Journal of Communication*, 56, 728–753. DOI: 10.1111/j.1460-2466.2006.00317.x. 71

Schudson, M. (1997). Why conversation is not the soul of democracy. *Critical Studies in Mass Communication* 14(4), 1–13. DOI: 10.1080/15295039709367020. 32

Schuler, D. (1994). Community networks: building a new participatory medium. *Communications of the ACM*, 37(1), 38–51. DOI: 10.1145/175222.175225. 13

Schuler, D. (1996). *New Community Networks: Wired for Change*. New York: ACM Press. 14

Schweitzer, E. J. (2008). Innovation or normalization in e-campaigning? A longitudinal content and structural analysis of German party websites in the 2002 and 2005 national elections. *European Journal of Communication*, 23(4), 449–470. DOI: 10.1177/0267323108096994. 52

Semaan, B., Faucett, H., Robertson, S. P., Maruyama, M., and Douglas, S. (2015). Designing political deliberation environments to support interactions in the public sphere. *Proceedings of CHI'15: The 33rd Annual ACM Conference on Human Factors in Computing Systems*. New York: ACM, 3167–3176. DOI: 10.1145/2702123.2702403. 37, 40, 59

Semaan, B., Faucett, H., Robertson, S. P., Maruyama, M., and Douglas, S. (2014). Navigating imagined audiences: Motivations for participating in the online public sphere. *Proceedings of CSCW'14: The 18th ACM Conference on Computer Supported Cooperative Work*, New York: ACM, 1158–1169. DOI: 10.1145/2675133.2675187. 60, 71

Sethi, R. J. (2017). Crowdsourcing the verification of fake news and alternative facts. *Proceedings of HT'17: The 28th ACM Conference on Hypertext and Social Media*, New York: ACM Press, 315–316. DOI: 0.1145/3078714.3078746. 79

Shah, D. V., Cho, J., Eveland, W. P., Jr., and Kwak, N. (2005). Information and expression in a digital age: Modeling Internet effects on civic participation. *Communication Research*, 32, 531–565. DOI: 10.1177/0093650205279209. 39

Shapiro, M. and Hemphill, L. (2014). Policy-related communications and agenda setting: Twitter, New York Times, and the Widening Soapbox. *Midwest Political Science Association National Conference*, Chicago, IL, April 3–6. DOI: 10.2139/ssrn.2585126. 54, 55

Shen, D., Sun, J.-T., Yang, Q., and Chen, Z. (2006). Building bridges for web query classification. In *SIGIR* (2006), 131–138. DOI: 10.1145/1148170.1148196. 56

Shim, D. C. and Eom, T. H. (2008). E-government and anti-corruption: Empirical analysis of international data. *International Journal of Public Administration*, 31, 298–316. DOI: 10.1080/01900690701590553. 74

Shim, D. C., and Eom, T. H. (2009). Anticorruption effects of information and communication technology (ICT) and social capital. *International Review of Administrative Sciences*, 75, 99–116. DOI: 10.1177/0020852308099508. 74

Shirky, C. (2011). The political power of social media technology , the public sphere , and political change. *Foreign Affairs*, 90 (February), 1–12. Retrieved from http://67.192.45.82/ASSETS/CD85D3ADA91B42BAB28C7B7C1E42ABEC/ForeignAffairs-1521.pdf. 7

Shklovski, I., Palen, L., and Sutton, J. (2008). Finding community through information and communication technology in disaster response. *Proceedings of CSCW'08: The ACM Conference on Computer Supported Cooperative Work*, New York: ACM Press, 127–136. DOI: 10.1145/1460563.1460584. 66

Silver, D. (2004). The soil of cyberspace: Historical archaeologies of the Blacksburg Electronic Village and the Seattle Community Network. In D. Schuler and P. Day (Eds), *Shaping the Network Society: The New Role of Civil Society in Cyberspace*, (pp. 301–324) Cambridge, MA: MIT Press. 14

Smith, K. A. (1987). Newspaper coverage and public concern about community issues: A time series analysis. *Journalism Monographs*, 101. 41

Smith, A. (2011). 22% of online Americans used social networking or Twitter for politics in 2010 campaign. Pew Internet and American Life. Available at: http://www.pewinternet.org/~/media//Files/Reports/2011/PIP-Social-Media-and-2010-Election.pdf. 55

Snow, D. (2004). Framing processes, ideology, and discursive fields. In D. Snow, S. Soule, and H. Kriesi (Eds.), *The Blackwell Companion to Social Movements*, Blackwell Publishers Ltd. DOI: 10.1002/9780470999103. 66

Song, I., Larose, R., Eastin, M. S., and Lin, Carolyn, A. (2004). Internet Gratifications and Internet Addiction: On the Uses and Abuses of New Media, *CyberPsychology and Behavior*, 7, 384–394. DOI: 10.1089/cpb.2004.7.384.

Sotsky, J. (2013). Pulling back the curtain on civic tech. Knight Foundation. Available at: https://knightfoundation.org/articles/pulling-back-curtain-civic-tech. 21

Soukup, C. (2006). Computer-mediated communication as a virtual third place: Building Oldenburg's great good places on the world wide web. *New Media and Society*, 8(3), 421–440. DOI: 10.1177/1461444806061953. 32

Stafford, T. F., Stafford, M. R., and Schkade, L. L. (2004). Determining uses and gratifications for the internet. *Decision Sciences*, 35, 259–288. DOI: 10.1111/j.00117315.2004.02524.x.

Starbird, K. and Palen, L. (2010). Pass it on? Retweeting in Mass Emerency, *Proc. of ISCRAM Conference*. 44

Starbird, K. and Palen, L. (2011). "Voluntweeters": Self-organizing by digital volunteers in times of crisis. *Proceedings of CHI'11: The ACM Conference on Human Factors in Computing Systems*, New York: ACM Press, 1071–1080. DOI: 10.1145/1978942.1979102. 66

Starbird, K. and Palen, L. (2012). How will the revolution be retweeted? Information diffusion and the 2011 Egyptian uprising. *Proceedings of CSCW'12: The ACM 2012 Conference on Computer Supported Cooperative Work*. New York: ACM, 7–16. DOI: 10.1145/2145204.2145212. 44, 63, 64

Starbird, K., Palen, L., Hughes, A., and Vieweg, S. (2010). Chatter on The Red: What hazards threat reveals about the social life of microblogged information, *Proceedings of CSCW* (2010), 241–250. DOI: 10.1145/1718918.1718965. 64

State, B. and Adamic, L. (2015). The diffusion of support in an online social movement: Evidence from the adoption of equal-sign profile pictures. *Proceedings of CSCW'15: The ACM Conference on Computer Supported Cooperative Work*. New York: ACM, 1741–1750. DOI: 10.1145/2675133.2675290. 67

Steitz, M. and Quinn, L. (2007). *An Introduction to Microtargeting in Politics*. New Politics Institute. 54

Stenberg, C. W., Ayres, Q. W., and Kettinger, W. J. (1983). Information technology and models of governmental productivity. *Public Administration Review*, 43(6), 561–566. DOI: 10.2307/975924. 15

Stones, R. (2005). *Structuration Theory*. Basingstoke: Palgrave-Macmillan. DOI: 10.1007/978-0-230-21364-7. 43

Stoycheff, E. and Nisbet, E. C. (2014). What's the bandwidth for democracy? Deconstructing internet penetration and ctizen attitudes about governance. *Journal of Political Communication*, 31(4), pp. 628–646. DOI: 10.1080/10584609.2013.852641. 3

Strang, D. and Soule, S. (1998). Diffusion in organizations and social movements: From hybrid corn to poison pills. *Annual Review of Sociology*, 24, 265–290. DOI: 10.1146/annurev. soc.24.1.265. 44

Stromer-Galley, J. (2000). Democratizing democracy: Strong democracy, US political campaigns and the Internet. *Democratization*, 7(1), 36–58. DOI: 10.1080/13510340008403644. 50, 53

Stromer-Galley, J. (2003). Diversity of political opinion on the Internet: Users' perspectives. *Journal of Computer-Mediated Communication* 8(3). DOI: 10.1111/j.1083-6101.2003. tb00215.x. 59, 70

Stromer-Galley, J. (2014). *Presidential Campaigning in the Internet Age*. New York: Oxford University Press. DOI: 10.1093/acprof:oso/9780199731930.001.0001. 48, 52, 53

Stroud, N. J. (2008). Media use and political predispositions: Revisiting the concept of selective exposure. *Political Behavior*, 30(3), 341–366. DOI: 10.1007/s11109-007-9050-9. 3

Stroud, N. J. (2010). Polarization and partisan selective exposure. *Journal of Communication*, 60(3), 556–576. DOI: 10.1111/j.1460-2466.2010.01497.x. 70

Suh, B., Hong, L., Pirolli, P. and Chi, E. H. (2010). Want to be retweeted? Large scale analytics on factors impacting retweet in Twitter network, in *IEEE Intl Conference on Social Computing*, IEEE, 177–184. 44

Sun, E., Rosenn, I., Marlow, C., and Lento, T. M. (2009). Gesundheit! Modeling contagion through Facebook News Feed. *Proceedings of the 3rd International Conference on Weblogs and Social Media*. 44

Sundar, S., Kalyanaraman, S., and Brown, J. (2003). Explicating website interactivity: Impression formation effects in political campaign sites. *Communication Research*, 30, 30–59. DOI: 10.1177/0093650202239025. 57

Sunstein, C. (2002). The law of group polarization, *The Journal of Political Philosophy* 10(2), 175-195. DOI: 10.1111/1467-9760.00148. 69

Sunstein, C.R. (2007). *Republic.com 2.0*. Princeton University Press, MA. 3

Sunstein, C. (2008). The law of group polarization. In J. S. Fishkin and P. Laslett (Eds.), *Debating Deliberative Democracy*, Blackwell Publishing Ltd. 70

Sveningsson, M. (2015). "It's only a pastime, rally": Young people's experiences of social media as a source of news about public affairs. *Social Media and Society*, July–September, 1–11. DOI: 10.1177/2056305115604855. 76

Tang, G. and Lee, F. L. F (2013). Facebook use and political participation: The impact of exposure to shared political information, connections with public political actors, and network structural heterogeneity. *Social Science Computer Review*, 31(6), 763–773. DOI: 10.1177/0894439313490625. 49, 50

Tedesco, J. C. (2004). Changing the channel: Use of the Internet for communicating about politics. In L. L. Kaid (Ed.), *Handbook of Political Communication Research* (pp. 507–532). Mahwah, N.J.: Erlbaum. 48

Tocqueville, A. (1969 [1835, 1840]). *Democracy in America*. (J. Mayer, Ed., and G. Lawrence, Trans.) Garden City, NY: Anchor Books. 36

Tolbert, C. J. and McNeal, R. S. (2003). Unraveling the effects of the internet on political participation? *Political Research Quarterly*, 56(2), 175–185. DOI: 10.1177/106591290305600206. 50

Tolbert, C. J. and Mossberger, K. (2006). The Effects of E-Government on Trust and Confidence in Government. *Public Administration Review*, 66(3), 354–369. DOI: 10.1111/j.1540-6210.2006.00594.x. 74

Tufekci, Z. and Wilson, C. (2012). Social media and the decision to participate in political protest: Observations from Tahrir Square. *Journal of Communication*. 62(2), 363–379. DOI: 10.1111/j.1460-2466.2012.01629.x. 7

Tufekci, Z. (2008). Grooming, gossip, Facebook and MySpace: What can we learn about these sites from those who won't assimilate? *Information, Communication and Society*, 11(4),544–564. DOI: 10.1080/13691180801999050. 40

Tumasjan, A., Sprenger, T. O., Sandner, P. G. and Welpe, I. M. (2010). Predicting elections with Twitter: What 140 characters reveal about political sentiment, *Proceedings of the Fourth International AAAI Conference on Weblogs and Social Media*. Association for the Advancement of Artificial Intelligence, 2010, 178–185. 60

Turcotte, J., York, C., Irving, J., Scholl, R. M., and Pingree, R. J. (2015). News recommendations from social media opinion leaders: Effects on media trust and information seeking. *Journal of Computer-Mediated Communication*, 20, 520–535. DOI: 10.1111/jcc4.12127. 60

Ubaldi, B. (2013). Open government data: Towards empirical analysis of open government data initiatives, OECD Working Paper, Public Gov. p. 61, 2013. DOI: 10.1787/5k46b-j4f03s7-en. 18

Uldam, J., and Vestergaard, A. (2015). Introduction: Social media and civic engagement. In J. Uldam and A. Vestergaard (Eds.), *Civic Engagement and Social Media: Political Participation beyond Protest*. Springer. DOI: 10.1057/9781137434166_1. 62

United Nations (2013). Department of Economic and Social Affairs: Guidelines on open government data for citizen engagement. Available at: http://workspace.unpan.org/sites/Internet/Documents/Guidenlines%20on%20OGDCE%20May17%202013.pdf. 18

Valenzuela, S., Park, N., and Kee, K. F. (2009). Is there social capital in a social network site?: Facebook use and college students' life satisfaction, trust, and participation. *Journal of Computer-Mediated Communication*, 14(4), 875–901. DOI: 10.1111/j.1083-6101.2009.01474.x. 3

van den Besselaar, P. and Beckers, D. (2005). The life and death of the great Amsterdam digital city. In P. van den Besselaar and S. Kaizumi (Eds.), *Digital Cities III. Information Technologies for Social Capital: Cross-cultural Perspectives* (pp. 66-96). Lecture Notes in Computer Science, 3081, Berlin: Springer-Verlag. DOI: 10.1007/b107136. 12, 13

van Dijk, J. A. G. M. (2005). *The Deepening Divide: Inequality in The Information Society*. Thousand Oaks, CA: Sage Publications. 73

van Dijk, J. A. G. M. (2012). Digital democracy: Vision and reality. In I.Th.M Snellen, M. Thaens, and W.B.H.J van de Donk (Eds.), *Public Administration in the Information Age: Revisited* (pp. 49–62). Amsterdam: IOS Press. DOI: 10.3233/978-1-61499-137-3-49. 11, 73

van Dijk, T. A. (2001). Critical discourse analysis. In D. Schiffrin, D. Tannen, and H. Hamilton (Eds.). *Handbook of Discourse Analysis*, Oxford: Blackwell Publishers, 353-371. 64

van Dijk, T. A. (2006). Politics, ideology and discourse. *Elsevier Encyclopedia of Language and Linguistics*, 2005. Volume on Politics and Language (R.Wodak, Ed.), 728–740. DOI: 10.1016/B0-08-044854-2/00722-7. 64

van Liere, D. (2010). How far does a tweet travel? Information brokers in the Twitterverse. *Proceedings of MSM'10: The International Workshop on Modeling Social Media*. New York: ACM Press. DOI: 10.1145/1835980.1835986. 44

Vargo, C. J., Basilaia, E., and Shaw, D. L. (2015). Event versus issue: Twitter reflections of major news—A case study. *Communication and Information Technologies Annual—Studies in Media and Communications*, 9, 215–239. DOI: 10.1108/S2050-206020150000009009. 41

Varol, O., Ferrara, E., Ogdan, C. L., Menczer, F., and Flammini, A. (2014). Evolution of online behavior during a social upheaval. *Proceedings of WebSci'14: The 2014 ACM Conference on Web Science*. New York: ACM Press, 81–90. DOI: 10.1145/2615569.2615699. 7

Vitak, J. (2012). The impact of context collapse and privacy on social network site disclosures. *Journal of Broadcasting and Electronic Media*, 56(4), 451–470. DOI: 10.1080/08838151.2012.732140.

Vitak, J., Lampe, C., Gray, R., and Ellison, N. B. (2012). "Why won't you be my Facebook friend?": Strategies for managing context collapse in the workplace. *Proceedings of the 2012 iConference* (iConference '12). ACM, New York, 555–557. DOI: 10.1145/2132176.2132286. 38

Vitak, J., Zube, P., Smock, A., Carr,. C.T., Ellison, N., and Lampe, C. (2011). It's complicated: Facebook users' political participation in the 2008 election. *Cyberpsychology, Behavior, and Social Networking*, 14(3). DOI: 10.1089/cyber.2009.0226. 7, 50

Voida, A., Dombrowski, L., Hayes, G. R., and Mazmanian, M. (2014). Shared values/conflicting logics: Working around e-government systems. *Proceedings of CHI'14: The ACM SIGCHI Conference on Human Factors in Computing Systems*, New York: ACM Press, 3583–3592. DOI: 10.1145/2556288.2556971. 3

Waddell, P., Millard, D., and Saunders, C. (2014). "stop g8": an ethnographic account of web use in global justice activism. *Proceedings of WebSci'14: The 2014 ACM Conference on Web Science*. New York: ACM, 269–270. DOI: 10.1145/2615569.2615647. 67

Wahid, F. (2012). The current state of research on eGovernment in developing countries: A literature review. In H. Scholl, M. Janssen, M. Wimmer, C. Moe, and L. Flak (Eds.), *Electronic Government*, vol. 7443, (pp 1–12), Berlin: Springer. DOI: 10.1007/978-3-642-33489-4_1. 18

Wallsten, K. (2007). Agenda setting and the blogosphere: An analysis of the relationship between mainstream media and political blogs. *Review of Policy Research*, 24(6), 567–587. DOI: 10.1111/j.1541-1338.2007.00300.x. 41

Wallsten, K. (2010). "Yes We Can": How online viewership, blog discussion, campaign statements, and mainstream media coverage produced a viral video phenomenon. *Journal of Information Technology and Politics*, 7(2–3), 163–181. DOI: 10.1080/19331681003749030. 42

Wallsten, K. (2011). Many sources, one message: Political blog links to online videos during the 2008 campaign. *Journal of Political Marketing*, 10(1–2) 88–114. DOI: 10.1080/15377857.2011.540203/.

Walther, J. B., Van Der Heide, B., Kim, S. Y., Westerman, D., and Tong, S. T. (2008). The role of friends' appearance and behavior on evaluations of individuals on Facebook: Are we known by the company we keep? *Human Communication Research*, 34, 28–49. DOI: 10.1111/j.1468-2958.2007.00312.x. 40

Wang, C., Medaglia, R., and Jensen, T.B. (2016). Mobilizing Government: Inter-Organizational Collaboration Using Open Social Media Platforms. *Proceedings of the 17th*

International Digital Government Research Conference on Digital Government Research (dg.o '16), Yushim Kim and Monica Liu (Eds.). ACM, New York, 357–365. DOI: 10.1145/2912160.2912177. 19

Wang, D. (2008). The idle and the busy. Teahouses and public life in early twentieth-century Chengdu. *Journal of Urban History*, 26(4): 411–437. DOI: 10.1177/009614420002600401. 29

Wang, Y. and Mark, G. (2013). Trust in online news: Comparing social media and official media use by Chinese citizens. *Proceedings of CSCW '13: The ACM Conference on Computer Supported Cooperative Work*, New York: ACM, 599–610. DOI: 10.1145/2441776.2441843. 65, 79

Wanta, W. and Hu, Y-W. (1993). The agenda-setting effects of international news coverage: An examination of differing news frames. *International Journal of Public Opinion Research*, 5(3), 250–64. DOI: 10.1093/ijpor/5.3.250. 41

Wanta, W. and Ghanem, S. (2007). Effects of agenda setting. In R. W. Preiss, B. M. Gayle, N. Burrell, M. Allen, and J. Bryant (Eds.), *Mass Media Effects Research: Advances through Meta-analysis*, (pp. 37–52). Mahwah, NJ: Erlbaum. 41

Ward, S., Gibson, R., and Lusoli, W. (2003). Online participation and mobilisation in Britain: Hype, hope and reality. *Parliamentary Affairs*, 56, 652–668. DOI: 10.1093/pa/gsg108. 3

Warner, W. and Hirschberg, J. (2012). Detecting hate speech on the World Wide Web. *Proceedings of LSM 2012: The 2012 Workshop on Language in Social Media*, 19–26. 79

Weaver, D. H. (2007). Thoughts on agenda setting, framing, and priming. *Journal of Communication*, 57(1), 142–147. DOI: 10.1111/j.1460-2466.2006.00333.x. 41

Weber, I., Garimella, V. R. K., and Borra, E. (2012). Mining web query logs to analyze political issues. *Proceedings of WebSci '12: The 4th Annual ACM Web Science Conference*, New York: ACM Press, 330–334. DOI: 10.1145/2380718.2380761. 56

Weber, L. M., Loumakis, A., and Bergman, J. (2003). Who participates and why? An analysis of citizens on the Internet and the mass public. *Social Science Computer Review*, 21, 26–42. DOI: 10.1177/0894439302238969. 3

Weeks, B. E., Arde`vol-Abreu, A., and Gil de Zúñiga, H. (2015). Online influence? Social media use, opinion leadership, and political persuasion. *International Journal of Public Opinion Research* 29(2), 214–239. DOI: 10.1093/ijpor/edv050. 60

Weeks, B. E. and Southwell, B. (2010). The symbiosis of news coverage and aggregate online search behavior: Obama, rumors, and presidential politics. *HMCS* 13(4), 341–360. DOI: 10.1080/15205430903470532. 56

Welch, E. W., Hinnant, C. C., and Moon, M. J. (2005). Linking citizen satisfaction with e-government and trust in government. *Journal of Public Administration Research and Theory*, 15(3), 371–391. DOI: 10.1093/jopart/mui021. 74

Wellman, B. (2001). Physical place and cyberplace: The rise of personalized networking. *International Journal of Urban and Regional Research*, 25(2), 227–252. DOI: 10.1111/1468-2427.00309. 37

Wellman, B., Haase, A. Q., Witte, J., and Hampton, K. (2001). Does the internet increase, decrease, or supplement social capital? Social networks, participation, and community commitment. *American Behavioral Scientist*, 20(3), 436–455. DOI: 10.1177/00027640121957286. 5

Wensch, J. S., McCroskey, J. C., and Richmond, V. P. (2008). *Human Communication in Everyday Life: Explanations and Applications*. Boston, MA: Pearson. 56

West, D. M. (2004). E-government and the transformation of service delivery and citizen attitudes. *Public Administration Review*, 64(1), 15–27. DOI: 10.1111/j.1540-6210.2004.00343.x. 74

Williams, C. and Gulati, G. (2013). Social networks in political campaigns: Facebook and the congressional elections of 2006 and 2008. *New Media and Society*, vol. 15 no. 1 52–71. DOI: 10.1177/1461444812457332. 52, 60

Wojcieszak, M. and Mutz, D. (2009). Online groups and political discourse: Do online discussion spaces facilitate exposure to political disagreement? *Journal of Communication*, 59(1), 40–56. DOI: 10.1111/j.1460-2466.2008.01403.x. 71

Woodly, D. (2008). New competencies in democratic communication? Blogs, agenda setting and political participation. *Public Choice*, 134(1–2), 109–123. DOI: 10.1007/s11127-007-9204-7. 42

Wulf, V., Aal, K., Kteish, I. A., Atam, M., Schubert, K., Rohde, M., Yerousis, G. P., and Randall, D. (2013a). Fighting against the wall: social media use by political activists in a Palestinian village. *Proceedings of CHI'13: The ACM Conference on Human Factors in Computing Systems*, New York: ACM Press, 1979–1988. DOI: 10.1145/2470654.2466262. 7

Wulf, V., Misaki, K., Atam, M., Randall, D., and Rohde, M. (2013b). 'On the ground' in Sidi Bouzid: investigating social media use during the Tunisian revolution. *Proceedings of CSCW'13: The ACM Conference on Computer Supported Cooperative Work*, New York: ACM Press, 1409–1418. DOI: 10.1145/2441776.2441935. 7

Xenos, M. and Moy, P. (2007). Direct and differential effects of the internet on political and civic engagement. *Journal of Communication*, 57(4), 704–718. DOI: 10.1111/j.1460-2466.2007.00364.x. 49

Xenos, M., Vromen, A., and Loader, B. D. (2014). The great equalizer? Patterns of social media use and youth political engagement in three advanced democracies. *Information, Communication, and Society*, 17, 151–167. DOI: 10.1080/1369118X.2013.871318. 50, 60

Yagade, A. and Dozier, D. M. (1990). The media agenda-setting effect of concrete versus abstract issues. *Journalism Quarterly*, 67(1), 3–10. DOI: 10.1177/107769909006700102. 41

Yardi, S. and boyd, d. 2010. Dynamic debates: An analysis of group polarization over time on twitter. *Bulletin of Science, Technology and Society* 20, S1–S8. DOI: 10.1177/0270467610380011. 71

Yasuoka, M., Ishida, T., and Aurigi, A. (2010). The advancement of world digital cities. *Handbook of Ambient Intelligence and Smart Environments*, Nakashima, H., Aghajan, H. Augusto, J. C. (Eds.) Springer-Verlag. 939–958. DOI: 10.1007/978-0-387-93808-0_35. 13

Zhang, W., Johnson, T. J., Seltzer, T., and Bichard, S. L. (2009). The revolution will be networked: The influence of social networking sites on political attitudes and behavior. *Social Science Computer Review*, 28(1), 75–92. DOI: 10.1177/0894439309335162. 55

Zhou, Z., Bandari, R., Kong, J., Qian, H., and Roychowdhury, V. (2010). Information resonance on Twitter: Watching Iran. *Proceedings of the First Workshop on Social Media Analytics*, ACM, 123–131. DOI: 10.1145/1964858.1964875. 60

Zuiderwijk, A., and Janssen, M. (2014a). Open data policies, their implementation and impact: A framework for comparison. *Government Information Quarterly*, 31(1), 17–29. DOI: 10.1016/j.giq.2013.04.003. 18

Zuiderwijk, A., and Janssen, M. (2014b). The negative effects of open government data - Investigating the dark side of open data. *Proceedings of dg.o'14: The 15th Annual International Conference on Digital Government Research*, 147–152. DOI: 10.1145/2612733.2612761. 18

Author Biography

Scott Robertson is a professor in the Information and Computer Sciences Department at the University of Hawai'i at Mānoa, where he currently serves as Department Chair. His academic background is thoroughly interdisciplinary, with an undergraduate degree in Social Science, a Master's degree in Cognitive Psychology, and a Ph.D. from a formative Cognitive Science program that combined psychology and AI. His early work was in the area of natural language processing, but he took a turn toward HCI after spending some time at IBM Watson Research Center. He has served as co-chair of the ACM Human Factors in Computing (CHI) conference (1995), the Digital Government Society conference (2014), and the EPIC Ethnographers in Industry conference (2018). His most recent research has been in the area of information and communications technologies as they influence civic engagement, focusing especially on social media and deliberation.